MICHAEL'S LEGACY

TRANSCENDING LIFE & DEATH

www.mascotbooks.com

Michael's Legacy: Transcending Life and Death

The use of titles (doctor, commander, admiral, pastor, father, shaykh, rabbi, swamy, etc.) is employed to clarify the role that some people highlighted in this book played in Michael's life. Others are referred to by their first names. This is not intended to minimize their importance as an individual or their relationship to Michael.

The cover design is a rendering of an original copyrighted photograph by Collette Fournier.

For more information, please contact:
Mascot Books
620 Herndon Parkway #320
Herndon, VA 20170
info@mascotbooks.com

CPSIA Code: PRFRE0720A
Library of Congress Control Number: 2020907161
ISBN-13: 978-1-64543-534-1

Printed in Canada

To Michael
who embodied the purest expression of kindness and love
and modeled it for all of us . . .

MARK JUDELSON

MICHAEL'S LEGACY

TRANSCENDING LIFE & DEATH

"*The purpose of life is not to be happy. It is to be useful, to be honorable, to be compassionate, to have it make some difference that you have lived and lived well.*"

—RALPH WALDO EMERSON

TABLE OF CONTENTS

PREFACE

The barking from the other side of the closed door sounded like it was coming from a large dog. I have a healthy respect for dogs in general, and large dogs in particular. You just don't know what's coming, and you can't really prepare for the unknown.

That was my state of preparation for this interview with Roxanne Watson. I was totally unprepared for the story that was waiting on the other side of the door.

When I asked my dear friend, Willie Trotman, to recommend people who had important stories that needed to be heard, Willie immediately responded, "Roxanne Watson" and gave me her telephone number. I wrote an occasional column for *Our Town*, a Rockland County (New York) newspaper. The column featured folks who are otherwise off the dominant culture radar screen and are committing acts of kindness and courage. Willie didn't tell me Roxanne's story and I didn't ask. Willie's recommendation was all that I needed.

I immediately called Roxanne and told her Willie suggested I call her for an article. Roxanne said, "If Willie is recommending it, I'll do it. Come on over." She gave me her address and we agreed on a date and time for the interview. The extent of my preparation was charging the battery of my phone (that I record interviews with), making sure that my pen had ink, and that there were blank pages in my notebook.

After Roxanne relocated her large dog, she opened the door and invited me in. We sat down. I asked her why she thought Willie had recommended her and out came a story that changed my life . . .

Roxanne's story had certainly changed her life. Seven years earlier, she had been near death at the age of fifty-six from heart failure. She was an inpatient in the Intensive Care Unit of Montefiore Hospital in Manhattan. She was waiting for a heart or to die.

During her hospitalization, Michael Bovill, a twenty-three-year-old member of the United States Coast Guard, crashed on his motorcycle on the George Washington Bridge. Three days later, Michael was declared brain dead. Michael was signed up to be an organ donor, and his parents also gave their consent for his organs to be recovered and transplanted. What had been Michael's heart was surgically transplanted into Roxanne's chest cavity where her failing original heart had just been removed.

As Roxanne told me her story, the hair on the back of my neck stood up. To say that I was moved is a monumental understatement.

I write and perform stories that reveal themselves to me. The test for whether I'll work with the story is if the hair on the back of my neck stands up.

At the end of the interview, I promised Roxanne to do justice to her story and that she would be the only person I'd show it to until and unless she gave me permission to share it with others. Happily, Roxanne gave me approval to go forward and the article was published.

But the story was not through with me. I told Roxanne that I wanted to speak with Michael's parents as I sensed there was much more to tell.

Roxanne directed me to Julia Rivera, director of communications at LiveOnNY, the agency that oversaw the recovery and transplanting of Michael's organs. Julia contacted Michael's parents, John and Jilayne Bovill, to relay my request. They quickly gave Julia permission to share their contact information with me. When I called their home, John warmly invited me to come for an interview. About ninety-eight percent of my life takes place within three miles of where I live. As I age, leaving this comfort zone has become more and more of a challenge. The projected ninety-minute drive—which normally I would avoid—barely caused a blip on the radar screen. As John and Jilayne told me their stories, the hair on the back of my neck stood up. I wrote their chapter and knew there was so much more to be revealed. They gave me contact information for their daughter, Mandy, who had been the closest of Michael's siblings in age to Michael. Mandy agreed to an interview—and my hair stood up.

I called the Coast Guard station at Eaton's Neck on Long Island where Michael had been stationed at the time of his death (and where he was heading at the time of his accident). The Coast Guardsman who answered the phone put me in touch with their public affairs officer. He put me in touch with Michael's station commander, Chief Warrant Officer Stephen Pollock, and roommate, Stephan Attzs. Mr. Pollock put me in touch with Admiral Joseph Vojvodich, who had met and been tremendously impressed with Michael. As I interviewed each of them, my hair stood up.

Every step of the way, the story confirmed its importance; confirmed the value of being told; confirmed that in all corners of the world, in all sorts of people and circumstances, there is kindness, generosity, and love; confirmed that Michael Bovill was a stellar model of a good human being and that it was my job to record and propagate his personal story and the larger story of the ripples of his gifts.

As Michael's story revealed itself, the stories of Roxanne's fellow recipients of what had been Michael's lungs, liver, and kidneys demanded their voice. The stories of their family members and clergy demanded their voice. The stories of the surgeons, physicians, and transplant coordinators demanded their voice. With the assistance of LiveOnNY, I made contact with many of the people directly impacted by Michael's legacy.

And throughout, the hair on the back of neck stood up.

INTRODUCTION

The heart beating in Roxanne Watson's chest originally beat in the chest of Michael Bovill. Roxanne refers to Michael as "my donor." Since receiving her transplant, Roxanne's mission is to sign up organ donors—which is what she was doing when a Spanish-speaking woman approached her. Roxanne (who speaks English but not Spanish), was staffing a table at a community health fair in the Bronx. Sitting next to her on the table was a framed photograph of Michael, which Roxanne literally carries with her everywhere she goes. In the photograph, Michael's head and chest are visible. When he died, Michael served in the United States Coast Guard as a firefighter and was training to be a helicopter mechanic. In the photo, he is wearing his dress uniform. Despite his military bearing, the faint hint of his ever-present smile is evident. When the Spanish-speaking woman approached Roxanne, she picked up the photograph of Michael. "It looked to me as if she wanted to take it with her," Roxanne said. "I received the photograph on the Oprah Winfrey television show when I met John and Jilayne [Michael's parents] for the first time." Roxanne held onto the photo and found someone who spoke English and Spanish. She explained to the woman that this was a photograph of her donor and it was precious to her.

She asked the woman, "Why do you want the photograph?"

The woman responded, "Because he's an angel." (The woman, in her early eighties, accepted Roxanne's ownership of the photograph. Roxanne happily recalled that she also signed up to be an organ donor.)

Michael's Legacy is the true story of Michael; his family; his Coast Guard shipmates; the five recipients of his heart, lungs, liver, and kidneys and their families; the doctors who recovered and transplanted those organs; other doctors who treated the recipients and the people of LiveOnNY; and the agency who made this awe-filled, technological wonder possible.

PART ONE

MICHAEL'S PARENTS

Michael's parents, John and Jilayne, met with me in their home on a Sunday afternoon. They had just returned from church. I was excited to meet them and hear about Michael from the two people who knew him best. At the same time, I wanted to respect their personal, intimate boundaries. We did not know each other, and I had not earned their trust. I was asking them to remove their armor and perhaps expose themselves and me to the greatest pain of their lives . . .

Michael Bovill was perhaps the fittest of the recruits in his Coast Guard boot camp. Where he could have finished first in most of the training exercises, he frequently finished tied for last. "He hung back to help the recruit who was struggling, run with them to encourage them," said his father, John. "That's who he was."

The day before he died in a motorcycle accident, Michael offered another example of his character. Twenty-three years old and on active duty with the Coast Guard, he was visiting his family for the weekend. Michael asked John for the keys to his mother's car. John recalled playfully saying to Michael, "You've got a motorcycle and a car! What do you need your mother's car for?" John smiled and continued. "Since he was in the Coast Guard, he called me 'Pops.' He said, 'Pops, just give me the keys.' So, I tossed him the keys. And do you know what he did? He filled the gas tank in his mother's car! That was Michael for you."

Michael's roots were embedded in Christianity. John's parents were officers with the Salvation Army, and then his father was led to be a Methodist minister. Michael's mother, Jilayne, grew up with her parents working for Teen Mission, a program where teenagers train and then go all over the world to perform missionary work. John and Jilayne met at a Teen Mission conference.

"We were staff kids together," John said. Their first meeting was not recognition of positive chemistry.

"It was the opposite," Jilayne said. "He was so conceited."

"I thought she was a goody two shoes," John said.

Four months later, they found themselves in the same school. John remembers thinking, "Wait a minute. I need to rethink this. She's pretty cool."

"His conceit was a little better. He was getting more mature," Jilayne said.

At the time, Jilayne was sixteen. John was seventeen. When Jilayne moved to Chicago to live with her sister, "John wrote me letters in these teeny tiny words," she said.

"A few months after she returned from Chicago, we decided to commit to each other," John said. "Four months later, we got married. It was 1985. If you know it's right, you know it's right." John was twenty-one. Jilayne was twenty. Michael was born May 3, 1987 and would be twenty-nine today. "Who could ask for anything better? Every dad wants a little boy to hang out with, to grow up with, to play ball with. His name came from the Bible. It means 'gift from God,'" John said.

"He was our gift," Jilayne said.

Michael's sister Mandy was born seventeen months later. "Her real name is Amanda but Michael couldn't say that and called her 'Manny,'" Jilayne said. "So we ended up calling her 'Mandy.' Then we decided to name all four of our children with the first letter 'M.'" Michael's sister, Marissa, was born four years after Mandy, and Madilyn was born two years later.

"Michael and Mandy were extremely close," John said. "He was the big brother who would bust out for his sisters." When Michael and Mandy were young children, John was building the family home and the kids spent hours with him. "I remember giving Michael a hammer and nails and he'd spend hours pounding them in any scrap wood. He was three years old and I hoped he wouldn't smash his fingers. He loved building stuff," John said. "It was a good way to hang out with your kids."

Michael's relaxed nature was evident early in life. "When we took him to the dentist," Jilayne said, "the dentist said, 'I wish we could bottle what Michael has and give it to other kids.'"

John continued. "He was a loveable kid with an amazing personality. He had the biggest smile you'd ever want. Very compliant. I loved hanging out with him."

"Always had that energy—very kinetic," Jilayne said. "Wanted to use his hands with everything—building, drawing."

In 1998, the Bovills decided to work for Christian retreats, which led them to the Shepherd of the Ozarks located in a rural area of northern Arkansas. "We had five hundred acres," John said. "Living the rustic life. Beautiful place. What a great place to raise our kids and teach them hard work ethics. I remember when Michael was fourteen, seeing him drive a bulldozer up the mountain. We had thirty head of horses. He was a pro at training them, breaking them. It was part of what we called our 'Horse Mission.' Our kids developed common sense. You had to think on your feet. We didn't have TV or cell phones."

Jilayne homeschooled her four kids for the five years they lived there. They often lost power in the winter and resorted to staying warm from fires in the wood stove. "We learned to survive and had a blessed time together. Developed our kids' characters," John said.

Michael grew up fascinated by firemen. Jilayne remembered him as a toddler, barely tall enough to see out the window, watching for the fire trucks of the nearby station to pass by. "His first word was 'ruck. He couldn't say truck," she said. "It came out ''ruck.' He'd call out, "Ruck, 'ruck, 'ruck Mommy!' He always wanted to be a fireman."

He attended junior college in Pocahontas, Arkansas where he studied fire science. In his second year, he was a member of the local fire station. "He loved it," John said. "Then we got a call to come to northern New Jersey to run a little retreat center on Schooley's Mountain. Michael hadn't graduated yet. He stayed in Arkansas to complete his studies. We left in December of 2006. He graduated in May of 2007."

Soon after he graduated, Michael packed up and moved to his parents' home in New Jersey. "His dream was to be a fireman either in New Jersey or New York," John said. "He pursued it. It was very political; very difficult to get in. Michael's cousin, Gus, was in the Coast Guard. They were close. Gus told Michael he could be a fireman in the Coast Guard. He was excited about it. I remember watching the recruitment video with him. I said to him, 'That's you! You found your niche!' He made the plunge. He signed up in 2009 and headed off to boot camp." Michael was twenty-two. Prior to his enlistment in the Coast Guard, the Bovills recalled everyone always called their son "Michael." His Coast Guard shipmates called him "Mike."

Jilayne said, "He was always respectful. He'd always open doors for women. Always let people go in front of him."

While his parents remembered Michael as an essentially angelic child, I imagined there had to be moments or incidents when he was mischievous or foolish or ill-tempered. I asked John and Jilayne if Michael ever got in trouble.

"He did get in trouble in boot camp because you're supposed to be serious," John said. "He had a natural smile. He'd be reprimanded for smiling all the time. You could yell at him and he'd still have that smile on his face. Just the way he was. When we are living our life for God, God gives us the confidence to live. I believe Michael had a huge faith in the Lord. He was content with where God put him. When he was discouraged from smiling in boot camp, I didn't know if he could stop. He was mad that they didn't believe that this was who he was."

After Michael's death, John and Jilayne heard stories from his Coast Guard shipmates that Michael had never shared. "They told us that Michael was an encourager," Jilayne said. "Michael would rally them. Every morning in boot camp, they told us he said, 'We can do this!' One of the Coasties called him 'my cheerleader.'"

Michael's determination to be part of his team at boot camp revealed itself when all four of his wisdom teeth were pulled on the same day. He was given ibuprofen for the pain and relieved of his duties for that afternoon. He refused the break and continued training with his team. "He was so determined to get through," Jilayne said. "He didn't want to be held back. He wanted to graduate with his team, pain or no pain."

After completion of boot camp, Michael was assigned to the Coast Guard station at Eaton's Neck on Long Island.

The weekend he died—as he did many weekends—Michael came to his parents' home at the retreat center in Schooley's Mountain, New Jersey. "It was July and hot," John recalled. "Our favorite thing to do together was to take our dog, Pumpkin, and go swimming. He called and said, 'Hey Pops, I'm on my way home. Let's hang out and take Pumpkin swimming. We had such a beautiful day together. On Sunday, Mandy, Michael, Jilayne, and I attended church together. Michael played guitar in the praise and worship band on stage at church."

After the family returned home from church, Michael drove to the Bronx to buy a turbo motor for his Subaru Impreza. He came home and unloaded the motor. John said, "My mom was here for that weekend. She and Michael got to hang out. My mom tells me that Michael hugged her. She's like ninety pounds and he lifted her off the ground, playfully spun her around, just embracing her. That's the last memory my mother has of Michael. I was about to take my mom to her home in South Jersey and Michael said to me, 'Pops, I'm going to take my motorcycle back to the Coast Guard station. You take Nanny home in my souped-up car.' So, I did."

That evening, Jilayne and John attended a Bible study group. She said, "Michael usually went back to his base between four and six. It took two and a half hours from here to his base. He liked to be in bed by ten or ten thirty because he was up at five in the morning. John drove his mom to her home that night. Michael left later than usual because he wanted to see his sisters who were returning from a church trip that evening. I was still at Bible study. I was a leader, so I stayed to clean up. Michael called me and said he was about to leave, but would wait for me. I told him I'd be a while and not to wait. I said, 'We'll talk tomorrow when you get off work.' That was the last I talked with him." Her voice broke. She paused to collect herself.

I deliberately lowered my gaze. I felt that Jilayne needed a degree of privacy and by looking away, I could give her some space. She was a mother re-living her last contact with her beloved son. She struck me, however, as wanting to go through it. John sat quietly. After a moment, she continued.

"So, he left, and riding his motorcycle back to his base, he had his accident." (The circumstances of Michael's crash are unclear. John said that the Port Authority investigated and thought it was a hit and run but that nothing was ever proven. What is known is that Michael's motorcycle went down on the highway on the George Washington Bridge and his head struck something.)

"That last weekend was just magical," John said. "The hug with his nanny; taking communion together; and for me, having that time, just him and me and swimming with our dog, catching up on life, how his work is going. We talked about his job, his career. We always dreamed about having a piece of property in Pennsylvania and having horses together."

After Michael left to return to his base, Jilayne waited for his call to alert her of his safe arrival:

He always called if he was going to be late or anything. If he didn't call, he would text because he was going straight to bed. That night he never called or texted. He left about nine thirty and should have gotten back by eleven thirty or midnight which was very late for him. All the girls and I had called him and called him. Mandy said the last time she called him, it was about one thirty [in the morning]. I got a call at three thirty in the morning asking if this is Mrs. Bovill. I said, "Yes." It was a lady saying, "Your son has been in an accident." She said she was at Harlem Hospital and "We're doing everything we can for him." I said, "What does that mean?" She said, "We're doing everything we can for him." That's all she would say. I asked for her phone number because I needed to call John. I wrote down where it was, the phone number, and hung up and called John. Then I got the girls up. I told them, "Michael's been in an accident and I'm going to the hospital. You can stay home and start praying."

Jilayne began crying and continued.

"The girls all insisted on going. In fifteen minutes we were gone. On the way there, I had to drive because if I didn't drive, I'd be going crazy. You have to be in control somewhere. I had Mandy call people to pray. On the way, we saw a detour on the George Washington Bridge. Mandy said, 'That's probably Michael's accident.' We got to the hospital about five fifteen on Monday morning."

"After Jilayne called me at my mom's house," John said, "I called the hospital and got the same message they gave Jilayne: 'We're doing everything we can.' I woke up my sister and told her I was going to Harlem Hospital. She woke up her husband. My mom, my sister, and her husband all went with me. We got there about an hour after Jilayne and the girls."

"That hospital was such a secure place—it looked like a prison," Jilayne said. "All shut up, no open doors anywhere, police officers standing at some of the doors guarding prisoners who were patients. When we got off the elevator on the fifteenth floor, I remember the hallway and I thought, *Where are we?* Empty hallway and closed doors everywhere. We found Michael. To see him that was so shocking. His nose was bleeding. Blood coming out of his eyes. Blood in his ears. Tubes hooked up to him."

Michael was not conscious. He was operated on that Monday. There was a large blood clot in his brain. Three hundred cubic centimeters of blood were removed. "The surgeons wanted to prove . . . if they relieved the pressure from the brain, got all that out, just needed to see if the brain was going to come back, and it didn't," Jilayne said.

"As believers, we prayed for the best possible outcome," John said. "We prayed for healing. Within twenty minutes of the completion of surgery, Jilayne had a vision of Jesus holding Michael in his arms. Simultaneously, John reported, 'I heard God say, 'Michael is with me.' We told each other what had happened. We had peace then. We knew he wasn't going to come back. That's the power of God. He is our belief."

"The neurosurgeon told us, 'I believe that at the moment of impact, Michael was gone, that he went to heaven,'" John said.

When the Coast Guard found out about Michael, at least ten of his comrades in full uniform arrived at the hospital. The hospital rules state that that only two people could visit at a time. With Jilayne's arrival, they numbered four. John arrived with three others. Then the boyfriend of one of Michael's sisters came. Then their pastor. Then the Coast Guard shipmates. The hospital rules were superseded by a higher authority.

Two Coast Guard shipmates stood at attention at the door to Michael's room the entire time Michael was in the hospital. John cried as he said, "One of the Coasties told us, 'Mr. and Mrs. Bovill, you go to my apartment and rest. We're going to stand here and watch over your son. You go and get some rest.' He stayed on base while we used his apartment. That was for three nights. The camaraderie during those three days . . . to get to know those guys. The commander was there. He was there almost twenty-four hours."

I felt tears in my eyes and a lump in my throat as John cried; Michael's comrades comforting their friend's parents, standing guard over their injured friend, remaining vigilant and present for Michael even though they had no idea whether he was aware of their presence and John's gratitude—it moved me deeply.

On Monday or Tuesday (the Bovills don't remember), representatives of LiveOnNY, New York State's official organ transplant agency, met the Bovills at the hospital. "We were still in shock so they came back the next day," John said. "When they asked us if we would allow Michael to be an organ donor, in unison, Jilayne and I said, 'Yes!' That's what he would have wanted. Later, we found out that he had signed up to be a donor and that was on his ID. They kept us informed about when they were going to harvest his organs."

For three days after the surgery, Michael was on life support. On the third day, the doctors declared him brain dead.

The Bovills returned home on Thursday. "When they told us that he was brain dead, that's when we felt comfortable to leave," John said. "It's over. They harvested his organs Friday, July 16, [2010]."

On Saturday, July 17th:

- Roxanne Watson, fifty-six, received Michael's heart
- Scott Tappet, thirty-two, received both of Michael's lungs
- Diana Martinez-Moran, seven, received Michael's right kidney
- Elijah Parker, eighteen, received Michael's left kidney
- Zhou Yuan Li, sixty-one, received Michael's liver

The youth pastor from the Bovills' church made arrangements for Michael's funeral. He had seen how many people came to the funeral home and recognized that their church was too small to accommodate all those people. He found a bigger church. More than four hundred people attended Michael's funeral.

The Coast Guard held a private ceremony for Michael and invited his family to attend. It took place on Long Island Sound aboard a Coast Guard ship. They spread his ashes in the Sound. "It was a rainy morning," John recalled. "When it came time to release his ashes, there was a separation in the clouds and a ray of sunshine came down."

A few weeks after the funeral, Admiral Joseph Vojvodich, the sector commander of the Coast Guard, came to visit the Bovills. Their first contact was a phone call from the admiral. John remembered him saying, "You don't know me, but I met your son." When he became the sector commander, he visited all the Coast Guard stations under his command. When he was at Eaton's Neck, the commanding officer of the station assigned Michael to be the admiral's driver. They spent part of a day together.

On a Sunday afternoon, Admiral Vojvodich drove from Washington, D.C. to the Bovills' home in northern New Jersey. "He sat in our living room and told us the impact Michael had made on him," John said. "He said, 'I wish every one of my recruits has the energy that Michael had. He was coming along so fast. He was learning so quickly. He had the motivation to learn the maps, language, skills. He was blossoming.'" Admiral Vojvodich told the Bovills that he put Michael on the list for the fast track for advancement. Michael never revealed this to his parents. He only said that he had escorted the admiral.

The following November, Chief Warrant Officer Stephen Pollock, the commanding officer of Michael's Coast Guard station, invited the Bovills to join them for Thanksgiving. Mrs. Bovill told Chief Warrant Officer Pollock, "We'd like to help with the dinner. We brought the pies. Twenty pies!" In the command center, Michael's ping pong paddle and baseball glove were displayed next to a photograph of him in uniform. There was also a sculptural memorial which incorporated an anchor on the grounds of the base.

"This tragedy crosses all the barriers," John said. He continued:

I embraced Roxanne as a lifelong sister. The color of her skin [Roxanne is African American. The Bovills are white.] did not mean one thing to me. I knew my son's heart was beating in her. I was so happy to embrace her. To put my ear against her chest and hear that beautiful sound, to know that life continued. Roxanne is a true testimony to what an organ recipient can be. It's emotional for an organ recipient and members of the donor family to meet. For us, it was a beautiful journey with friendship and love that crossed all barriers of race and religion. Roxanne is creating a wonderful legacy. She's signed up almost nine thousand organ donors. It's not in vain that your loved one passed because their life makes it possible for others to have life. That's what it's all about: that he gave life so that others could have life. Same with Scott—couldn't walk from the hospital bed to the bathroom without getting out of breath. Scott asked our permission to name his daughter after Michael. They gave her the Hebrew name Michaela. We were so happy. They're Jewish and we were invited to attend the naming ceremony at their synagogue.

It was attended by ninety family members and friends. We sat in the front row. The rabbi spoke about how God delivered the Israelites out of Egypt all the way to Michael giving Scott the lungs to breathe so that his daughter may have life. Michael gave life to Scott. Scott continues to give life. So beautiful. We can ask for no more. Some people never know why a loved one had to pass. We believe God pulled back the curtain of heaven and said, "Let me share a little bit why I took your son." We got to meet Roxanne. We got to meet Scott. We got to meet Elijah and Zhou. To see life giving life. It's just incredible. We gave life to Michael, but as we named him, we knew he was a gift from God. We pledged all our kids to the Lord. Ultimately, they were God's. Michael wanted to warm others' hearts.

For Jilayne, the ownership of what had been Michael's organs is simple, "I think those organs that were given to people were Michael's," she said. "And now, those organs are theirs. Their life. They're given a chance to continue to live. It's Roxanne's heart now. It was a gift given to her. I know it was my son's heart. But now it's her heart. She's the one who's living with that heart. It's about life everlasting. They're living because of Michael. God gave us a life. Why not share it? I tell people that God needed Michael more in heaven to glorify God more than he was needed on earth."

I hadn't known what to expect when I left my home earlier in the morning. All that I knew was that this was a story I was called to tell. Michael's parents were remarkably willing to open their hearts and memories, both joyous and profoundly painful. I felt grateful for their generosity and found myself feeling love for Michael and knowing Michael's legacy was just beginning to reveal itself to me.

MICHAEL'S SISTER

Mandy Bovill loved her brother. "He was definitely my best friend in the whole world," she said. "We did everything together. We got along really well. Even when we were teenagers and into our early twenties, we stayed best friends. We texted all the time. We talked every day. We talked about everything together. You name it—we talked about it. Right before his accident, we were planning to get an apartment together near New York City. But obviously, our plans didn't make it that far."

She recalled a game they played as little children when they lived in Florida. "We called the game 'Gators' because there were alligators all around. In our living room, we set up pillows in the gaps between the couches and jumped from one to the other. We were 'safe' if we only touched the pillows or couches but if we touched the floor, the gator would eat us. Michael was the gator. To make it harder, he'd chuck pillows at our feet to try to make us trip and fall." Mandy feels this was Michael's playful way to help her and her sisters be quicker. "I always felt Michael's love trumped all."

Mandy emphasized Michael's dedication to his faith.

He was a goofball, for sure, but he was definitely a devoted follower of Christ. We took our faith very seriously. He wasn't pushy about it. He didn't make people feel uncomfortable. He had this overwhelming love. Some of his friends from the Coast Guard called him "the modern day Jesus." It was kind of a joke but he was so giving and loving, so caring and kind, that it was real, too. People were drawn to him because of how he carried himself. Michael was so easy to get along with, to be friends with. He was so genuine. He didn't need to go out and evangelize. His actions spoke louder than his words. He didn't have to push his faith on other people. He was just kind and loving. That's what he believed God wanted him to be. And that's what he was. He was so strong in his faith that he didn't have to throw that on anybody. That love came from the Lord. He strived to be the person he believed God wanted him to be.

Mandy reported that one of Michael's enduring qualities was his smile. Mostly, people who met Michael experienced him and his smile as genuine and welcoming. She remembered that his smiling, however, got him in trouble. After joining the Coast Guard, he went through boot camp. "The company commanders [drill instructors] gave him a hard time about his smile," she said. "They thought he was mocking them, that he was a smart aleck. They made him do extra push-ups or extra runs as punishment. It's just he couldn't contain his smile. He always had a smile on his face."

"The night of Michael's accident, I worked late closing the restaurant where I was a waitress," Mandy said.

He left ten minutes before I got home. I was really sad to miss him. When we didn't hear from him, my sisters and mom and I kept texting and calling him, but we didn't hear anything back. It was very weird because we always received a response from him. He always called or texted to let us know that he got back. I had a concern, but I tried not to let my concern get the best of me. I was just like, "He'll text us in the morning. He'll call us in the morning." My sisters and I were hanging out in my room. When we got a response from Michael they would go to bed in their room. So, while we were hanging out, we listened to music. We always listen to music. About eleven thirty, this beautiful piano song came on and we were like, "That's such a pretty song." It was "Kiss the Rain." The piano player was Yiruma. I said, "If I ever die, I'd want this to be played at my funeral because it's such a pretty song." It was weird that we had that conversation the night of his accident which we think happened about ten thirty or eleven. At his funeral, we played that song.

I went to sleep around two o'clock. My mom got a call from Harlem Hospital about three or three thirty in the morning. She woke us up and told us that Michael had been in an accident. As soon as I heard, I went into protective mode to protect my sisters. We had to get up quickly to go to the hospital. I said to my sisters, "Hospitals are cold. You have to bring sweaters." Our dad had taken his mom to her home in South Jersey so he wasn't there. I had to take on the role that my father did to protect my siblings. Maybe I had this subconscious feeling that he was just gone and we weren't going to see him again, that he was never going to be with us again. When we got to the hospital, I had this overwhelming feeling that he wasn't there anymore. I knew his physical body was there, but he just wasn't there. It was devastating. It was horrible.

I always have peace about where he was. I had no doubt that he was in a better place, that he wasn't suffering, that he wasn't in pain, that he's happy with the Lord. His accident was utterly devastating. It was so heart-wrenching but sometimes, I feel like a hand on my shoulder. There's no physical presence but in the spiritual realm, he is there. I feel it's the Lord reassuring me that he's okay and that I'll be okay without him. It was hard for me when I got married that my best friend wasn't there. I have no idea what he's doing now, what job God has for him. I know that whatever he's doing, it's full of love. I'm one hundred percent sure that his job when he was alive was to save people. He always wanted to help people, to save people. After he died, a mutual friend told me that Michael had once told her, 'I want to do everything I can to save people.' That goes hand-in-hand with the 'modern day Jesus' nickname he had. Jesus came to give his life to save us. That's what Michael did. Before he joined the Coast Guard, he was a firefighter. He loved it. He also worked in landscaping. He'd always bring coworkers home with him, giving them a place to eat or stay if they needed that. Even when we were little kids, he was always trying to help us, encouraging us to do better. We had thirty horses when we were in Arkansas. We trained them—what people call 'breaking' horses. It's a hard process. He'd always encourage me, telling me, "You're doing such a good job. Keep going." It's what he did. It's why he joined the Coast Guard—so he could help people. He was training to be on helicopters to do search and rescue missions. The motto of the Coast Guard is Semper Paratus which means "always ready." That was Michael's mission—always ready to help someone else. He was always ready to save people, to help people. When he was a landscaper, we got a lot of snow in North Jersey. He was always, always out there plowing people's driveways, to plow people out of the snow. He was always ready.

When I was a young girl, I had insecurity issues. He told me, "You're such a perfect person. If I ever marry or date someone, I would want her to be like you." I took that with me wherever I went. I can smile bigger now because of the way my brother treated me. I can laugh a little bit harder because I know that my brother told me that I was a good person. I miss him so dearly.

JOHN FANNING

MICHAEL'S SENIOR PASTOR

P astor John Fanning's strongest recollection of Michael was his smile. "Pastor John," as he is known to his congregants, was senior pastor of the church where Michael and his family were faithful and active members.

Michael's smile was his shining characteristic. He lit up a room when he came in. He had a great smile, a really contagious, infectious smile; a great personality. He was a winsome person. He drew people to himself. Not because he was a showoff. It was the warmth of his personality. You couldn't help but like the guy. He was a very warm and happy guy.

When Pastor John spoke about Michael's funeral, he noted the large presence of joy that was expressed and experienced by those attending. "The funeral was a reflection of Michael's spirit, his brightness, this smiling charismatic individual. That joy is what Michael would have wanted at his funeral."

Pastor John knew Michael from the time his family moved

from Arkansas to New Jersey. It was three or four years before his accident.

I was the pastor of Valley View Chapel in Long Valley. So I was pastor to Michael and his family. All the Bovills regularly attended Valley View Chapel. I helped them with their spiritual needs. I counseled them from time to time and visited when there was sickness. We had a number of young adults in the church who were his age. He was very close to four or five of them.

Michael was interested in motorcycles and fast cars. "He loved motorcycles," Pastor John said. "It was one of his first loves."

Michael is almost exclusively remembered for his kindness, playful nature, and smile. Pastor John remembers one incident —specific to his mechanical inclination—where he came off as less than angelic, but still with redeeming qualities. The incident related to Michael's love of restoring and customizing cars. He had a particular affinity to Subaru. Pastor John recalled:

Michael had fixed up a Subaru into kind of a hot rod. I can tell you [laughs] about the one time I had to speak a bit harshly to Michael. He and a couple of his friends were up at the church in what I believe was his car. We had had a snowstorm. There was snow and ice in our large parking lot. I was in the church and looked out my window and saw this car racing around the parking lot doing figure eights and 360s and sliding around. I go out into the parking lot and wave at the driver who I believe was Michael. I just shook my head and said, "Hey Michael, that's not a good idea." He gave me his winsome smile and said, "Okay." That was a funny thing that happened between me and Michael. It was typical of him. He was a fun-loving guy.

Michael regularly attended church. He participated in our program for young adults. He was very much involved in that. He played lead guitar in our church band which performed during our services. From what I could observe, he had a consistent faith and the church was a very important part of his life.

On the day of Michael's accident (Sunday, July 10, 2010), Pastor John remembered that Michael and his family attended services.

He was on leave for the weekend and was visiting his family. We had Communion Sunday on that day. Michael took communion with his family. At the end of the service, I was standing by the door greeting someone. Michael didn't stand in line to shake my hand, but I remember looking at him, nodding at him, and him nodding back at me and his smiling and he was gone. That was the last time I saw him alive. I saw him every day in the hospital but I'm not sure he was alive at that point.

Early on the morning of Monday, July 11th, Pastor John learned of Michael's accident. He received a phone call from Joshua Dean, the youth pastor of his congregation.

Josh told me, "Michael Bovill has been in a terrible accident. He's in Harlem Hospital." I said to Josh, "Let's go," and we rode together to the hospital. It was a desperate situation. Michael was in a coma. Perhaps he was brain dead at that point. I'm not sure. Michael was hooked up to a ventilator and a lot of other machines and IVs. John [Michael's father] and I were standing next to Michael's bed and I said to him, "You know, John, I don't think Michael is here. I think Michael is with the Lord. I think the Lord has taken the spirit away from the body. The hospital is keeping his body alive."

John said to me, "Jilayne and I had the same conversation that we don't think Michael is alive." I don't know why I said it. I don't have any special powers to know whether someone is alive or dead. I didn't say it to comfort them. I just had this

*feeling that Michael was gone. He might have been gone from the
moment of the accident.*

*I remember the presence of the Coast Guard at the hospital.
That was unbelievable. Uniformed members of the Coast Guard
were there twenty-four hours a day. They were doing what they
could for the family.*

For the next three days, Pastor John drove from western New
Jersey to Harlem Hospital. He said he stayed in the hospital for
seven to nine hours each day.

*Pastor Josh was there all the time, too. There were at least a dozen
of Michael's friends from church who were there almost all the
time. They were camped out in the hallway. So much so, that the
hospital staff got kind of irritated that there were so many people
in the hallway that they asked some of them to go downstairs
and wait. So, they rotated and took their turns. That was three
days of waiting for something to happen.*

*John and Jilayne were in the room with Michael a lot and
I didn't want to intrude on that. I think I went into Michael's
room only two times. I was there when John and Jilayne needed
me. Once or twice a day they came to me to ask for prayer.
I was happy to oblige. We prayed for wisdom, for the doctors,
for sensitivity, and compassion for the staff. We prayed for
comfort for everybody who was in the hospital, for the Coast
Guard, for their safety in their jobs.*

*It's interesting to me that I never once did I pray for
Michael's healing. For some reason, I just didn't feel like that
was the plan. I did pray if Michael is alive that he be conscious
of the Lord's presence, conscious of comfort, and confident in his
eternal destiny. But mostly, I prayed for comfort for the family.
I prayed for the strength to get them through this tremendous
ordeal. It seemed to give them health and hope. Michael was so*

critically injured that it didn't seem to be in the will of God that he be healed.

John's mother was there, too. She was in her late seventies or early eighties. She was a very sweet lady. For some reason, I took on the responsibility of being her companion. I would sit with her in the waiting room. My job was to comfort her. I remember the last day we were there and John and Jilayne came into the waiting room where John's mother and I were sitting. They said to her, "We're going to say our last goodbye to Michael." They had decided at that point that he was gone and had given permission for his organs to be donated. They asked Grandma if she wanted to go in and she said, "No. I don't think I'm up to it." I said to her, "Would you like me to stay here with you?" and she said, "Yes, would you please?" So I had the privilege—and I mean that, the privilege—of sitting with her. That was my mission.

People recognized that the funeral could not take place at Valley View Chapel as their seating capacity was about two hundred people and that many more were expected. They made arrangements with a neighboring church that had a larger seating capacity. Pastor John estimates three hundred to four hundred people attended the service. (The sermon he delivered at Michael's funeral is found at the end of this chapter.)

One of the attendees was the commandant of the Coast Guard. Pastor John said, "This was the number one guy in the entire Coast Guard and he came from Washington, D.C. for the funeral. It meant a lot to Michael's family."

Pastor John spoke about what animated Michael.

Michael had a remarkable relationship with his sisters. They adored him and he adored them. He was so protective and loving. Perhaps his passing was more devastating to his sisters than to his parents. I remember that it was a very sad time because Michael was so young, but the service was joyous.

It was triumphant. John and Jilayne made it that way. They could have taken a very different attitude. They made the service a very joyful time. They were sad that their son was gone but they had a hope that carried them through. The hope came from their belief that Jesus Christ rose from the dead. And because of his resurrection, those who place their faith in Christ as their Savior—when they die—will go to Heaven to be with the Lord. And we all believe in the resurrection of the body from the dead when the body is reunited with the spirit and we will live forever. They believed that Michael was in a better place. He was spared a lot of the suffering of a normal life and they believed that he was more alive at that moment than he ever was in his life. I believe it was their confidence that Michael's faith carried him to heaven. It wasn't the end for them. They believe they're going to see him again when their time on earth is done. The whole family believed that. His parents and sisters and Jilayne and John's families—they all believe that. The separation is temporary. It's not permanent in their minds, in our minds. That was what gave them hope. I did funerals many times of people who did not have that hope and it is a totally different atmosphere. It's one of despair and tears and just unbridled grief. There was sadness (at Michael's funeral) but not to that degree.

Pastor John and his wife have both signed up—on their drivers' licenses—to be organ donors.

We thoroughly believe in that. It breaks our hearts that there are people waiting for organs who are going to die before they get them." He said that in his church, there is no religious teaching one way or the other specific to organ donation and transplants, but he draws some principles from Jesus' saying, *"Do unto others as you would have them do unto you."*

I think one of the things that really comforted John and Jilayne, and indeed all of us, was the knowledge that Michael was such a healthy young man and there were people who were helped, whose lives were saved because Michael donated his organs. That was a source of great comfort. It was like a part of Michael is living on in the lives of those five people. He didn't die for nothing.

When Pastor John learned that the recipients of Michael's organs are of different faiths, he said:

It is just wonderful. We're all human beings. We may differ in our religious point of view. We may even believe in a different God. I happen to believe, John and Jilayne and Michael all believe in Jesus Christ as the Lord and Savior. But if someone doesn't believe that, it is totally irrelevant as far as organ donation is concerned. The Bible says to love your neighbor as yourself. Who is your neighbor? It is defined as anybody who you have the capacity to help. Religion has nothing to do with it. Suppose someone is an atheist and doesn't believe in God at all. And they needed a kidney, they needed a heart, and I or a loved one was in the position to give them life—absolutely! The religious aspect of it from the standpoint of organ donation is totally irrelevant. We're all human beings. We need to help each other.

Pastor John and the Bovills are members of a denomination called the Christian and Missionary Alliance. They have missionaries in more than thirty countries. "We believe that the Bible is the word of God," said Pastor John.

We use the Bible as our rule of faith and practice for what we believe and how we behave. We believe that Jesus Christ is the son of God, that he came to earth because humanity needed to be rescued from the penalty of our sins. He died on the cross in our place to pay the penalty of our sins with his blood. He rose from the dead and he ascended to heaven and all who believe in Christ and his death and resurrection have the assurance of eternal life. We also believe that Christ himself in the form of his holy spirit lives inside of us and helps us to recognize right from wrong and to live the kind of life that is kind and gracious and helpful and hopefully productive.

I was impressed with how Pastor John modeled doing what you can do to be of service where you are in the moment of need. At the hospital, he recognized that Michael's grandmother was the person who most needed the comfort he could provide. He took on being her companion during that trying time after the accident. And he was there when John and Jilayne needed his prayers.

There is this ongoing theme in my life that I was seeing played out in Michael's legacy:

Do what you can do with the resources at hand.
To be of service.
In the place where you are.
In the moment of need.

These qualities—unique to person, time, and place—became a regular presence in the stories of Michael and those whose lives he touched. . .

FUNERAL SERMON FOR MICHAEL BOVILL
July 20, 2010
Washington Assembly of God
Washington, New Jersey
Delivered by Pastor John Fanning

This has been a tough nine days. For some of you, it's been the hardest nine days of your lives. For those who knew Michael best and loved him most, you never thought it would be like this. You never thought you could feel such pain and loss. Your loved ones and friends have watched you suffer. We've stood with you. We've cried with you. We've done what we could to come alongside you yet realizing that the burden you've carried since you got the news that Michael was in the hospital is so heavy that even all of us put together can't lift it from your shoulders.

I've been a pastor for over thirty-six years. I've preached a lot of funeral sermons. In one sense it's never easy to preach a funeral sermon. But when a man or woman has lived a long and fruitful life—when they have raised their children, enjoyed their grandchildren, and their work on earth is clearly done and there is every advantage to their arrival at their eternal home—then a funeral sermon is pretty easy to preach.

But that's not the case today. It's not the case today because *in our eyes* we weren't supposed to be at a funeral service today for a handsome, young military man with his whole life—so full of possibilities and potential—stretched out before him. We sense that something's "out of kilter." This isn't *right*. It must all be a dream and we'll wake up soon and life will be as it was on the morning of July 11th.

The book of Job tells the story of man who suffered greatly. In fact, he suffered so much that the name "Job" is synonymous with suffering beyond description.

We're told in Job 1:18-19, "While he was still speaking, another messenger arrived with this news: 'Your sons and daughters were feasting in their oldest brother's home. Suddenly, a powerful wind swept in from the wilderness and hit the house on all sides. The house collapsed, and all your children are dead. I am the only one who escaped to tell you.'"

Job had three friends who heard about his pain. They wanted to visit their friend. Job 2:11-13 tells us that:

> When three of Job's friends heard of the tragedy he had suffered, they got together and traveled from their homes to comfort and console him... When they saw Job from a distance, they scarcely recognized him. Wailing loudly, they tore their robes and threw dust into the air over their heads to show their grief. Then they sat on the ground with him for seven days and nights. No one said a word to Job, for they saw that his suffering was too great for words.

Job's suffering was "too great for words." For a week, they just sat and cried with him.

Finally, Job gave vent to his anguish and frustration. He said that his pain was so great, his wounds were so deep, that he wished he had never been born.

In response to his cry, his friend Eliphaz said:

> In the past you have encouraged many people; you have strengthened those who were weak. Your words have supported those who were falling; you encouraged those with shaky knees. But now when trouble strikes, you lose heart. You are terrified when it touches you. Doesn't your reverence for God give you confidence? Doesn't your life of integrity give you hope?

In other words, "Job, you tried to comfort sorrowing people. You encouraged them to trust in the Lord. Now that tragedy has hit close to home, don't you believe your own words?"

Curiously, his friend's words were true, but Job didn't need the unvarnished truth that day. He needed a hug. He needed sensitivity. He needed a non-judgmental friend who would understand that it's not the time for *words*. The pain was too fresh.

That's why a pastor who preaches a funeral sermon on an occasion like this is in a tough spot. Those whose hearts are breaking today don't need *words*. Yet I've been asked to deliver a funeral message. So I need to put some words together. My hope and my prayer are that my words would be touched by God and that they would comfort, encourage, and if need be convict those of us who are here today because we love Michael Bovill.

So what's a preacher to say at a time like this?

Last Thursday morning, the day after I went to Harlem Hospital for the final time, I read my Bible. Lately I've been reading Psalms, and last Thursday I came to Psalm 78. Psalm 78 is a long psalm—seventy-two verses. Before I read a scripture passage, I pray and ask God to show me one or two or three verses that apply to me and what I'm going through. Then I take a few minutes and I write about what those verses seem to be saying to me. Then I try to meditate on those thoughts at various times throughout the day. When I finished reading, reflecting, and writing, I knew that I had something to say to the family and friends if I were asked to preach at Michael's funeral.

So I'm going to do something very personal. I'm going to read to you what I wrote in my journal last Thursday morning. Then after I share with you my "journal thoughts," I want to make one brief application.

The verses that the Lord wanted me to focus on last Thursday were Psalm 78:52, 53a, 72: "But he led his own people like a flock of sheep, guiding them safely through the wilderness. He kept them safe so they were not afraid . . . He cared for them with a true heart and led them with skillful hands . . ."

Here's what I wrote about those verses:

I have spent the last three days walking through the valley of the shadow of death with the Bovill family. Their son Michael has gone home to be with the Lord. A skeptic might say that the Lord did not guide Michael safely through the wilderness last Sunday night; that the shepherd failed to keep Michael safe as he rode across the George Washington Bridge; that He failed to care for him with a true heart; and that His hands were not skillful enough to keep Michael on his bike.

Everything that has happened since last Sunday night could be used to assault God's character. And it might even be accurate to say that even some of us who believe deeply in the promises of God question at times like this the wisdom, the care, and the love of God. The same psalmist who here praised God's loving heart had cried out in despair just one psalm earlier in Psalm 77:9 "Have His promises permanently failed? Has God forgotten to be kind? Has He slammed the door on His compassion?"

Then I read my selected verses once again: "But He led His own people like a flock of sheep, guiding them safely through the wilderness . . . He . . . led them with skillful hands."

Then I wrote:

Where was the good shepherd guiding Michael last Sunday night? Where was the good shepherd leading Michael with skillful hands last Sunday night? If it was to Station Eaton's Neck in Northport, Long Island, then God can be accused of falling down on the job. But that was not where God was guiding Michael last Sunday night. Skillful hands had no intention of leading him to Station Eaton's Neck.

Where was the harbor to which Michael Bovill was sailing? With skillful hands, the Lord Jesus brought him to his eternal port of call by way of the George Washington Bridge. From before Michael was conceived in his mother's womb, that was the good shepherd's plan.

God's GPS didn't fail on the night of July 11th. His skillful hands did exactly what they were supposed to do. They carried Michael safely to his heavenly home.

Author and speaker Ravi Zacharias told of being in the midst of a speaking tour when he was informed of his mother's death. Back in his hotel room, he said that he was tormented by two words that kept going through his mind: "She's gone! She's gone!"

Suddenly calm descended upon his wounded and broken spirit as he heard the still small voice of the Holy Spirit whisper, "*Gone where?*" He then realized that she had gone to a place called heaven and that she was in the presence of the Lord whom she had loved and worshiped.

It's only natural for those of us who loved Michael so much to say again and again, "He's gone!" But let's also take comfort in the answer to the question, "Gone where?"

How can you be assured that *you* have the promise of heaven? God has made it as simple as A, B, C, and D.

A: Admit that you have sinned and separated yourself from God. The Bible says, "All have sinned and fallen short of the glory of God." Your chances of getting to heaven by being good are equal to your chances of swimming from California to Hawaii in your own strength. We've all fallen short of God's glory.

Instead of comparing yourself to other people, compare yourself to God's law. Romans 3:20 says, "No one will be declared righteous in God's sight by observing the law; rather, through the law we become conscious of sin." You must humbly admit that you haven't kept God's law and that you are in need of his forgiveness.

B: Believe in Jesus Christ as your personal Savior. John 3:16 says, "For God so loved the world that he gave his one and only Son, that whoever believes in him shall not perish but have eternal life."

To believe is more than just saying, "I believe that Jesus is the son of God." It's putting your faith in his death on the cross to save you. It's placing your ultimate trust in him and not in yourself.

Admit you're a sinner, believe in Jesus, and C—confess Jesus as the Lord of your life. Romans 10:9 says, "If you confess with your mouth, 'Jesus is Lord,' and believe in your heart that God has raised him from the dead, you will be saved."

When Jesus Christ died for us, he died publicly on a hill outside the big city of Jerusalem on the busiest day of the year. He asks that when we make a decision to follow him, we confess him publicly, unashamedly.

In Matthew 10:32 Jesus said, "Whoever acknowledges me before men, I will also acknowledge him before my Father in heaven."

Admit that you're a sinner, believe in Jesus as your personal Savior, confess him publicly, and D—demonstrate your faith in Christ by repenting of your sins and receiving Christ into your life as your Forgiver and Leader.

Repentance means "to change direction." You've been living your way, so now live God's way. It doesn't mean you're going to live a perfect life from this point on, but it means you changed your direction and you're now going to follow Christ.

Receiving Christ means asking him to come and live inside of you so that you can be the kind of person you—deep down—want to be and the kind of person God created you to be.

I'd like to give you an invitation to receive Christ into your life today and begin a personal relationship with him, the same relationship with Christ that Michael had.

Jesus, I want to know you personally. Thank you for dying on the cross for my sins. I confess my sins to you right now and I open the door of my life and receive you as my Savior and Lord. Thank You for forgiving me of my sins and giving me eternal life. Take control of the throne of my life. Make me the kind of person you want me to be. *Amen.*

JOSHUA DEAN

MICHAEL'S YOUTH PASTOR

During a church-sponsored mission to Mexico, Michael's infectious brightness led his youth pastor, Joshua Dean (referred to as "Pastor Josh"), to call him a "pied piper." Pastor Josh led this trip bringing eight young adults from Michael's church in New Jersey to Ensenada, Mexico. When the church group arrived in Ensenada, a cement foundation had already been laid and the materials for the house were on site. They worked on the house during the mornings before the heat of the day set in. In their week's labor, they completed construction of a four-room house which included a kitchen, bathroom, and two bedrooms. Pastor Josh reported proudly, "We were able to hand over the keys to a finished house over at the end of the week."

In the afternoons, the church team brought food and drinks to a local park where they worked with young people who Pastor Josh referred to as "disadvantaged youth who didn't have safe and healthy homes." A portion of the afternoons was devoted to what Pastor Josh called the "soccer ministry." When the church group was about to return to New Jersey, Pastor Josh recalled:

There were two boys who Michael had done soccer ministry with and they were crying that Michael was leaving. The boys who Michael had befriended were about twelve or thirteen years old. They had known him for just one week and Michael made a huge impact with them. I think Michael was shocked that the boys were so attached to him. He said to me, "How am I going to get back to see them again?"

The seven days in Mexico demonstrated Michael's charisma to Pastor Josh:

Michael had a gift with children that is definitely rare. And that was so clear in Mexico. When we brought food and drinks to a local park and played with kids, Michael was so intentional to be with the kids. He learned their names and was always hanging out with them. Kids just loved being with him. That's why he reminded me of the Pied Piper. Kids can tell if the person leading them is excited or not. They sense if somebody really cares about them. Michael sang and danced with his whole body with the kids. He didn't care if some people thought he looked silly. It was the full-hearted way that he worshipped or led the kids. Sometimes, when the rest of us took a break, Michael played soccer or a ball game called four square with the kids. He was totally committed to sharing Jesus with the kids. He was deeply authentic. It was clear that he really influenced the rest of our team. When you have someone who really wants to be there and is giving one hundred percent of himself all the time, the others on the team get inspired, too. He was always thinking of others. During the construction, he was always the guy who I had to tell to take a break. Michael became the example for others on the trip for how to be. Always telling other people they were doing a good job. Always looking for the best in others. He also could make corrections by saying, "Hey man, you're trying so hard but you might want to try it this way!" I don't think Michael was fluent in Spanish, but he didn't let his lack of fluency get in the way of engaging with people. He communicated a lot with his body language, especially his smile.

Pastor Josh knew Michael for about three years before he died:

I was close friends with John (Michael's dad) as we were both in the ministry. We were kindred spirits and we lived on the same road. I met Michael at church. He became an active member of the young adults group of which I was pastor. I helped him get his first job in New Jersey with a friend from church who was employed at a landscaping company.

Members of the youth group were between the ages of nineteen and twenty-nine. Pastor Josh identified three purposes of the group.

The first was to worship together and spend time in God's word, providing mutual encouragement. The second was to serve. An example was the summer mission trip to Mexico where we spent a week building a house together. And the third was to share Christ's love with other people in our community. Sometimes we did this through service. Sometimes through having conversations with folks in coffee shops where we'd talk about our relationships with God. The group met on a weekly basis and we'd average between twenty-five during the school year and about seventy-five during the summer. I organized the worship, teaching, and service projects. We went to the beach and went bowling and had bonfires. Michael had friends through work who didn't necessarily have a relationship with Jesus or go to church. Through the group, we created safe environments for young people and their friends to experience what it means to be in a relationship with people who cared about Jesus and cared about them. He often invited friends from work to join us and they came.

Michael was very relational. He had the ability to make people feel that they were the only people he was talking to. It's a rare gift to be in a large group and to have the feeling that you're only talking to one person. Michael would focus on that one person. He asked questions and could listen in such a way that it gave the impression that you're the only person who matters in that moment. He didn't need to be around people all the time but when he was, he was very intentional. When he and I spoke, he made me feel I was the only person. He didn't ask questions that he thought he already had the answers to. He'd ask questions because he genuinely wanted to know. He responded in such a way that you knew he was really listening. He was a very gifted listener. He asked really good questions. Because he was so personable and genuine, he could ask questions that were personal without people getting offended. You could tell he really wanted to know you and understand you and how your world met up with his world. He was always looking for the best in people. He was always looking at the bright side. He was a trust-first, suspicion-later kind of guy. Only if that trust was not warranted would he engage in any kind of suspicion.

My experience of Michael was that his relationship with Jesus was deeply authentic. His relationship with God was not something that he did. It was something that he was. It was almost that it was part of his DNA. He had a deep knowledge of the Bible, but it was how Michael applied it to his everyday life that made him so special. He was always willing to participate and help with our worship. He was always willing to talk about his faith. He didn't do it because he was compelled to. He didn't do it because our church demanded. He didn't do it because the Bible tells you to. He did it because he believed it. His love of the Lord came out in his behavior and his actions. His faith was not part of his life. His faith was his life. Michael made

a decision that Jesus was going to be his only hope of Heaven.
That Jesus was going to be his only hope of forgiveness for the
sins he committed in his life. That Jesus was not going to be just
his Savior but also his Lord. He understood Jesus to be the son
of God, the Savior of the World. He understood that Jesus led a
perfect life on this Earth and that he died in order to take away
the sins of mankind. Jesus was not just someone to follow or just
believe. It was that Jesus was his friend, confidante, and the
guiding force in his life. Jesus was Michael's closest friend.

There's nothing you can do to earn the love of Jesus Christ
and there's nothing you can do to lose the love of Jesus. So Jesus
had a deep and profound love for Michael, in the same way he
has a deep and profound love for all the people he's ever created.
I believe the special way Michael applied his faith to his life must
have brought a tremendous joy to Jesus' heart. When you live
your life in accordance with God's word and when you live your
life with a desire to bring joy to Jesus, then you don't always have
to use words. Michael consistently exemplified Christ.

Early in the morning of July 11th, Michael's sister, Mandy, called
Pastor Josh to inform him of Michael's accident. Pastor Josh and his
colleague, Senior Pastor John Fanning, drove together to Harlem
Hospital. Pastor John drove. During the drive into the city, "I
was praying for Michael and his parents," Pastor Josh said. "And
then I felt that was God whispering into my heart. I felt Michael
was already with God. That Michael's spirit had already passed.
So, I had the opportunity to prepare myself for his passing."

When the pastors arrived at the hospital, Michael was on life
support. He wasn't breathing on his own. The medical staff was still
determining the extent of his injuries. "We weren't sure if Michael
was going to survive," Pastor Josh said.

I spent every day that week at the hospital to be there for the family. We knew the longer he was on life support the less likely he'd be able to recover. I remember walking into his room in the ICU and I did not recognize Michael at all. He was so badly hurt. If someone hadn't told me it was Michael, I wouldn't have known it was him. His body was filling up with fluids. His face was disfigured.

I spent most of the time in the hospital with the family trying to help them hold it together after they spent time with Michael, making sure they had something to eat and drink and a place to sleep. When I was with Michael, I talked directly to him open to the possibility of his being present and able to understand. I spoke as if he could hear me. I didn't know if he could consciously hear and understand what I was saying. I read Scripture to him. I told him how much I appreciated him and the way that he lived and cared for his family.

Pastor Josh officiated at Michael's funeral. The people attending included Michael's friends from the young adult group at church, station-mates from the Coast Guard, coworkers from his landscaping job, other friends, and family members. "It was a diverse and eclectic group of people," Pastor Josh said. "The one common denominator was their love and appreciation of Michael."

Pastor Josh reflected on his personal and theological beliefs regarding organ donations and transplants:

There is a verse in Scripture that says "to be absent from the body is to be present with the Lord." At the moment the spirit is taken from the body, I believe that person is transformed into the purpose of Christ. I consider the earthly body to be a gift from God for the time we have on earth. That we are to use that body well for the time God gives us. To use our time, our energy, our money well. They are all gifts from God. That's why we care for our bodies. That's why we don't do harmful things to our bodies. I believe while we're on earth, our bodies are the temple of the Holy Spirit. If we have a relationship with Jesus, we have the spirit of God inside our bodies while on earth. The moment we lose our lives, the moment our spirit departs from our body, our body is no longer our space to use. I don't have a strongly developed personal theology around organ donation or transplants. But in the context of what Michael went through, he was a young person who took good care of his physical body and chose to be an organ donor to pass on whatever parts of his body are helpful to someone else. That is good stewardship. It continues to steward the gift God gave you. In some ways, it's an example of the Gospel itself. That Jesus gave his life on behalf of the people of the world. It's what Michael did for the many people who benefited from his organs. From a personal standpoint, I feel that organ donation could be one of the Lord's ways of extending the lives of those who are still on this earth. It's an example of Christ himself and the sacrifices he made. I wouldn't say the Bible requires all Christians to be organ donors but I would say that as individuals choose to donate of themselves, I believe it is an example of the Gospel.

On a personal level, I think it's beautiful that the recipients of Michael's organs were of different genders, races, and religions from Michael. I think that Michael was able to extend the lives of people from all different walks of life is beautiful. They are all children of God. And I think that God would want them to extend their lives to give them an opportunity to know who God really is. The longer they are on earth, the higher the potential they have to know Jesus for themselves. I think it's pretty cool. And, yes, I'm signed up to be an organ donor.

Pastor Josh is the father of two sons and one daughter. He said, "I've often hoped and prayed that my oldest son become that type of big brother that Michael was."

ONE OF MICHAEL'S CLOSE FRIENDS

A t the end of a ten-hour workday fertilizing lawns, their last customer asked Andrew Kohlieber and Michael Bovill if they would caulk his two leaking skylights. Andrew, one of Michael's closest friends, remembered telling the older man, "No, we're working for the lawn service right now. We can't help with this other stuff."

They drove the truck to their company's yard and unloaded the supplies and equipment. At that point, Andrew thought he and Michael would drive home together. (They lived close to each other and carpooled to work.) That's when Andrew remembers Michael saying, "We should go back and help that guy. We're not at work anymore." Andrew agreed and they drove back to the customer's house.

"So, we knock on the guy's door and he was all happy. We didn't know how to caulk the windows, but Michael was willing to do it! So we had to figure out how. This was before smartphones, so we couldn't google it. But we did a good job. I went back for a year or two after and the skylights didn't leak," said Andrew.

Michael and Andrew met in 2007 after Michael graduated from fire school in Arkansas and joined his family in western New Jersey. They both were members of Valley View Chapel, and their youth pastor, Joshua Dean, asked Andrew to welcome the newcomer. Pastor Josh had also reached out to another member of the congregation who was a manager of the lawn service company—where Andrew already worked—to see if there was a job opening for Michael. There was.

Andrew was twenty and Michael was nineteen when they met for the first time. "It was right after a church service," Andrew said. "Michael was kind of quiet and reserved. I was a bit more eccentric so I led the conversation most of the time. He was polite and excited to start working at the lawn care company where I was at. The polite part didn't last that long after we got to know each other [laughs]."

In addition to being carpooling neighbors, coworkers, and active members of the same church, Andrew and Michael did many other things together:

> We'd work ten/twelve hours a day and after a while we'd hang out after work in the evening. We played a lot of ping-pong. We played video games. We rode motorcycles together. We were young and we rode fast occasionally [laughs]. We did wear helmets. He showed me some things on the guitar. He was really good at guitar. He tried to teach me how to play [laughs]. He was a good teacher but I was a terrible student [laughs] so that didn't last very long. He taught me the opening to "Dueling Banjos." It was the only song that stuck to my brain. He was patient as a teacher and he had a passion for guitar so he enjoyed playing and teaching.

"We talked about high school and some stories about his life in Arkansas. Sometimes, we'd joke around. I could be sarcastic but Michael wasn't. We talked about that. I meant my humor in a playful way."

About a month or two before his accident, Michael told Andrew that the Coast Guard could be tough and that he appreciated Andrew preparing him for the new culture.

One thing the two friends did not discuss was organ transplants:

We never spoke about transplants. I didn't know he had signed up to be an organ donor . . .

Sometimes we talked about religion. It was different talking with Michael than with a non-believer, a non-Christian. Michael was a true believer in Christianity. I shared that with him. He very much did what was right because that's what we're supposed to do and we're called to live that way. We were on the same page.

Michael was willing to help others out. Available if you needed him. He always stepped up to the plate. At the landscaping company, he'd be the first to do a task for someone who was tired or hot.

He had a huge grin almost all the time. He was hardly ever not smiling.

Michael's girlfriends were from the church. They typically were quiet. He was always very kind to them. Put them first. Very respectful of them. He was devoted to his sisters above pretty much everything else. The only times I saw him angry was when something negative happened to his sisters. If someone was mean to his sisters, he defended his family.

Andrew reflected on changes he saw in Michael when he joined the Coast Guard. "Before the Coast Guard, he was responsible. After joining, he was even more responsible. That means doing what you're supposed to do, doing the right thing. If he said he'd be somewhere at a certain time, he'd be there at that time."

Andrew learned about Michael's accident when he was getting ready for work on Monday morning, July 11, 2010:

It was six fifteen or six thirty. A friend called and said Michael was in an accident and in critical condition. I decide to go to the hospital right after work. I hang up the phone and get in my car to go to work. I just don't feel right. So I call work to tell them what happened but I couldn't talk at first. Emotion just swept over me. My brain was saying "Everything is going to be fine," but I didn't feel fine about it.

Andrew cried for more than minute, unable to speak.

The manager at work told me to take as much time as I need to be with Michael. So I went to the hospital. For the first day, we waited in the lobby because his family was with him in intensive care. We had a friend who lived pretty close by and we stayed at her house at night. We went back the next day. We were able to see him. [Andrew cries.] Pastor Josh took me into the ICU and I saw it was Michael but he wasn't recognizable. His whole body was really swollen. It took me a second to get that was him. It was hard. I loved Michael and he was badly injured. It was a shock. I did not speak to him. I couldn't touch him [cries]. It was too uncomfortable for me to touch him [cries]. We all left on the third day to give his family a chance to say goodbye.

After Michael died, I wondered why God would take this perfect person. At the time, I was going to school to become a physical therapist, but I fought it and fought it. Then one day, I came to the realization that Michael died when he was way too young—never done anything that was deserving of what happened to him. He had the opportunity in his life through his parents to cultivate a positive relationship with them and the church, with Christ. So, my wife and I dropped everything and moved to Indiana to work at a Christian boarding school. Since then, I've been involved in youth care—one hundred percent. That's a testament to Michael's relationship with me. Had I not known him, I wouldn't be where I am now—changing lives. It's quite a legacy he left with me. I'm working with juvenile justice trying to cultivate young adults with having at least one positive relationship. I work with troubled teens in an attempt to rehabilitate their behavior.

Michael always showed his faith by his actions. He never preached at anybody. Sometimes that's what people need. They don't need to be badgered. They just need to be shown compassion and all the good stuff will come. If I can do that for a couple of people, I'll feel pretty decent. What made Michael so special was his dedication and devotion to God. People would look at Michael and go, "I want what he has." He couldn't be anything but loving through Christ. Michael didn't preach the preaching. He lived the preaching. I remember this quote: "Preach Christ and when necessary use words." That to me was Michael. That's how he lived. I miss Michael every day.

ONE OF MICHAEL'S CLOSE FRIENDS

Michael Bovill spent much of the day of his fatal accident with his close friend Tom Legg and Tom's girlfriend (now wife), Michelle. According to Tom, he and Michael shared many passions, highest among them being God and Subarus. Michael's agenda for the afternoon of July 10th, 2010 was to pick up a used engine he had found online for his beloved Impreza RS near New York City. After Sunday services at Valley View Chapel, Michael, Tom, and Michelle ate lunch with Michael's dad at the church. Then the three friends drove Tom's father's Toyota RAV4 to get the engine—a turbo-charged WRX engine that was more powerful than the original one.

On the way into the city, Tom—who had been driving and reports that he "is not fond of big city driving"—turned the wheel over to Michael. Tom recalled:

> *Michael pulled up to a light and made a left onto a one-way road, except we were heading the wrong way! A stream of traffic*

headed straight toward us. I yelled, "Oh my God, we're going to die Michael!" Michael shrugged off this while laughing. He quickly off-roaded up onto the curb and we were all cracking up laughing. I can still remember the looks of the people in the cars passing us.

After purchasing and loading the engine, they were returning home when the muffler of their car fell off while they were driving on Route 80, a heavily trafficked highway. Tom asked, "What are we gonna do?"

Michael replied, "I know what we can do."

With traffic whizzing by, "We pulled off to the side of the road to make a temporary fix," Tom said. He continued:

We had a strap and quickly tied the exhaust up. A couple miles down the road the exhaust started dragging on the road again. I was about to hop out when Michael confidently said, "I got this," and went to make the repair. A few minutes later he walks to the side of the car as I rolled down the window. I asked him, "Do you need some help?" Michael looks at me and slowly lifts his hands showing us a six-inch piece of half-melted strap and says, "I don't think I can tie it back up." We all burst into laughter. Michael had a personality that could make the trials thrown at you become something joyful. Whatever life threw at him, Michael would charge ahead with a smile on his face and a lot of laughter.

We're almost home and Michael pulls in to get gas. Before he gets out of the car he looks back in the car at Michelle and me and says, "You guys are going to get married." Michelle and I had already decided that we wanted to marry but hadn't announced it. I said, "Michael you can't tell anyone. It's not official yet." Michael said, "Dude, I won't tell anyone. That's awesome! And, of course, you will name your son after me." I told him, "Well of course and you will make the best uncle!" I still feel that he was

saying, "Goodbye. You'll be fine without me." We unloaded the
engine and transmission at his parents' house. We went inside
for a few minutes and we shook hands, gave each other a big hug
because he had to go back to the Coast Guard station that night.

Early in the morning of July 11th, Tom got a phone call from
Michael's sister, Mandy, telling him that Michael had been in a
serious accident...

Tom and Michael met for the first time at a church barbecue.
"There was a bonfire and we talked about cars," Tom said.

I found out he was a Christian so we had those two interests in
common. We started hanging out. For the three years until he
passed, he and I were pretty much inseparable. We were Subaru
fellowship guys together. Michael had the biggest heart and the
biggest smile and energy and just a fire for enjoying life bigger
than any person I ever met. The girls loved him. He was a kind,
sweet man who brought happiness to everybody that he talked
to. He had this light and glow around him that seemed to stick
on the people he met.

The two were frequently joined by Tom's brother, Chris
Legg, and Chris Minerley who was always called "Minerley." The
four shared many car-related adventures. "One time there was a
drenching rain, and we had his car up on jacks," Tom said. "We
were upgrading the exhaust manifold in the middle of a rainstorm
because we had taken it apart before the storm hit. We were just
laughing, lying in the mud and putting it back together because the
car was the only way to get home. Michael made life interesting and
fun. Everywhere he went he always had a smile on his face."

Despite being a well-liked, admirable individual, Tom affirmed
that Michael was never one to boast about his personal successes
and friendly personality:

Michael was very humble, shy. He never would talk great about himself. He was one of the most kind and honest people I ever met. He changed my life. Before I met Michael, I knew people who were going down a path that I didn't want to follow. I didn't really have a good direction in my life. Meeting Michael brought me closer to God. Through Michael and the church, I found a group of friends, people who were downright there for you, who had your back, people who you knew would really be there for you even in really bad times. He brought me into that. He was like a brother. We did everything together.

One of their shared activities took place on many Friday nights. Tom, Michael, Chris, and Minerley drove together to the Delaware Water Gap. "It was our Friday night thing," Tom said. "We'd get off from work. We had free time. We'd go to the 7-Eleven for food and coffee and drive around exploring the roads. We'd sing. We'd be up until to two o'clock in the morning exploring the roads. We liked to listen to dancing music and country." Tom continued:

Michael was a great guitarist. Funny thing was he was a shy person who didn't like to be the center of attention. I would always tell him, "You're really awesome dude. You have such great skills. You're really awesome at playing the guitar." He'd always say, "No, I'm not." He'd put his head down and looked a little embarrassed because he didn't want to take any credit. I don't remember him playing solo. Somehow, I think because he was humble, people were drawn to him.

He loved to dance, to boogey. I found out from him that dancing was a lot of fun. He loved to give credit to other people. It made other people happy. He'd say to anybody, "Ah man, you're so good at this."

Tom explained their attraction to Subarus was their resemblance to trucks, which enables them to be driven fast off-road:

We were always off-roading in the dirt and mud. It was a lot of fun. He loved the rumble sound Subarus made. I loved the sound, too. My brother and I went to school to learn the auto mechanics trade. Michael didn't have an extensive knowledge about cars, but he picked it up fast and he loved to learn things. We switched engines and transmissions and put new clutches in. We put a better exhaust on his car. He put sport seats in his car. He loved his car. It was his baby. But cars were just a hobby for the four of us to spend time together and have a good time.

Michael was committed to whatever he engaged in. Tom reported that at the weekly church-sponsored volleyball game, Michael was very competitive. "He loved the game, and he gave it his all. And he was smiling while he played. He smiled when someone on his team made a good play, and he smiled when the other team made a good play. He almost never didn't have a smile on his face."

Because of Michael's genuine joy, which was visible through his magnetic smile, Tom said, "A lot of girls were attracted to him, but he was very shy. He was not a guy who played the field even though there were a lot of women who wanted to date him. He wasn't out to take advantage of anybody. He was looking for a woman who was into the stuff that he liked but who also is a godly woman, someone who believed in Christ."

Tom credits Michael for helping him strengthen his own faith:

People came to him for guidance. I came to him when I had trouble and I needed somebody to talk to. I felt I could tell him anything. He would support me. He might just listen. But when I needed it, he told me, "God is there for you," or he'd give me a pat on the back. You could be an open book with Michael and he'd never knock you down. He would do anything to build you up. You could take your armor off when you were around him. You didn't need a shield.

When I met him, I was not an avid church goer. My family had been involved with church on and off. So I had some experience with God, but when I met Michael I saw how church changed his life. He was very passionate about the Lord. He was so happy and I saw the light in that and it drew me to church and got me involved with the church's youth group. One of the reasons I know the Lord today is the influence he had on me.

On the night of Michael's accident, Tom was staying in the guest room at the home of Michelle's family. Around two o'clock that morning, Michael's sister, Mandy, phoned Tom and reported, "Michael's been in a motorcycle accident."

"My heart literally just sank," he said:

I was shocked. Michelle and I had just been with him during the day. I remembered a time about a year before. Michael and I had just left a church gathering. He was riding his motorcycle and I was following him in my car. He skidded off the road right in front of me. It scared me. Luckily, he was fine that time. But the phone call from Mandy—I knew it was something really bad that had happened. I took off work the next three days and Michelle drove me into the city to the hospital every day. At the hospital there were way more people than the hospital liked. Every day we waited for some good news to happen. Then we got news that he was brain dead. I was in the waiting room and I just broke down crying on my cousin's shoulder. It takes a lot for me to cry. I couldn't stop crying. I went into Michael's room and said goodbye. I felt like I was talking to a body instead of a person. I felt his presence was already gone. It was very hard. It affected me for a long time. I felt a bond with him that I have yet to re-create. It was like my brother died. There was a massive hole in my life.

Tom and Michael spoke about many things during their friendship, but they never talked about transplants. "But right after he died, I signed the back of my driver's license to be a donor."

During the service at Michael's funeral, Tom spoke about Michael's love for his family:

He always used to say to me, "If I die tomorrow, I'll be happy as long as my family is taken care of." When I spoke at his funeral, I told people that he said this all the time. So, I said at the funeral, "Just take care of the Bovills at this time because that's what Michael would have wanted." He loved his family. His family was everything to him. He loved his sisters. He loved his parents. He adored them. They meant the world to him. He told me so many times how much they meant to him.

He always wanted to save people. He wanted to help people. That's why he went to firefighting school. When he joined the Coast Guard, I felt it gave him a sense of purpose. He was in something for the greater good. He could help people by being in the Coast Guard in ways that he couldn't before.

A year after Michael died, Tom and Michelle got married. "Michael's whole family came to our wedding," Tom said. "I danced with his mom because I could see the sadness in her eyes. I love her like a mother. She was a second mother to me."

When asked to look back on Michael's legacy, Tom said, "The time I spent with him was one of happiest times of my life. He brought the goodness out of people. He had something in him that made people happy and smile. He will always hold a special place in my heart and mind. I can't wait until the day I get to be reunited with him in heaven."

CHIEF WARRANT OFFICER
STEPHEN POLLOCK

MICHAEL'S STATION COMMANDER

Despite meeting Michael Bovill only one time before Michael's accident, Stephen Pollock came away with a lasting impression. "I took over command of the base at Eaton's Neck (where Michael was stationed) in July," he said. "When I met him, I had been in the Coast Guard for seventeen years. Michael was coming down the stairs. Even though there was a difference in our respective ranks, he had the biggest smile on his face, shook my hand, and introduced himself. Super nice guy."

Michael's accident happened on a Sunday going into Chief Warrant Officer Pollock's first workday as the station commander. "My experience started with the phone call from the station's second in command, Wayne Valliet," he said. Officer Pollock continued:

Wayne called me about two forty-five Monday morning. He said Michael had been in an accident and that he was being taken to Harlem Hospital. I got off the phone and quickly met Wayne. We went to the hospital. That's where we met Michael's parents. We told them, "We're here for you." We stayed at the hospital all day long. It started out with just me and Wayne but then members of the crew started to show up. We had a thirty-two-member crew and by the end of the day, we set up a watch where we had two members of our crew stand outside Michael's door around the clock. He was never alone. We did that for four days and also when Michael was at the funeral home. I stood watch at the funeral home. There was a general sense with the crew that we weren't going to leave him alone. It was clear that the other members of the crew loved Michael.

"The mission of our station was to save lives," he said. "This meant search and rescue, maritime coastal security [defending against terrorist attacks], and recreational boating safety/law enforcement. The core mission is preventing the loss of life."

Except for a skeletal crew staffing the base, Officer Pollock and the rest of the station crew attended Michael's funeral. "One of the guys told about being with Michael in the shop after hours," he recalled.

Nobody else was around. They had to wear dry suits in which you're totally sealed so that no water can enter in case you fall in the water. There is a gasket around the neck and wrists. Michael stuffed the hose of an air compressor inside one of the seals and blew himself up like the [Stay Puft] Marshmallow Man. He said it was the funniest thing he ever saw. Everybody cracked up at the funeral.

Michael was what we call a good shipmate. He would be there for you. He never got in trouble. He was a good kid. This guy really lived life.

STEPHAN ATTZS

MICHAEL'S ROOMMATE IN THE COAST GUARD

Stephan Attzs had just completed boot camp when he met Michael Bovill. For Stephan, recently celebrating his nineteenth birthday, Michael might have represented a twenty-two-year-old seasoned veteran. Stephan was assigned to be Michael's roommate. "Michael had been at the station for a while when I got there," Stephan said. "He was a really cheerful guy. His smile was really big. I was just out of boot camp. He helped me loosen up."

The two were roommates for six months. "I never really had any serious talks with him," Stephan said. "He told me about his bike [motorcycle], his Ninja. We talked about the twenty-fives [the response boats the Coast Guard employed]. He never spoke about his religious beliefs."

Stephan was one of many of Michael's shipmates who came to Harlem Hospital after Michael's accident. He remembers being struck by how swollen Michael's face was. Despite Michael's appearance, Stephan expected Michael to recover. On Tuesday (two days after the accident), when Michael's parents informed Stephan and his Coast Guard shipmates that Michael was with Jesus and that he would not recover, "I was surprised," Stephan said. During the several days Michael was on life support at the hospital, shipmates kept a twenty-four-hour-a-day vigil standing guard over Michael. Stephan said while standing guard, "I was anxious. I was anxious the whole time I was there. While we were waiting, the shipmates were sad. I felt it was in God's hands."

Stephan attended Michael's funeral. "There were hundreds of people there. First time I saw something like that for someone who wasn't a famous person or a celebrity. He was a great person. It was like the whole town was there old and young people. Except for a skeletal crew remaining at Eaton's Neck, the whole unit was there."

ADMIRAL JOSEPH VOJVODICH

MICHAEL'S SECTOR COMMANDER

When Admiral Joseph Vojvodich met Seaman Michael Bovill, the admiral was in his twenty-fifth year of active service with the United States Coast Guard. Michael had less than a year of active service. "It was in June 2010," Admiral Vojvodich said.

I was incoming sector commander for a section of Long Island and Connecticut. Michael was assigned to be my driver to take me from Eaton's Neck [where Michael was stationed] to the station at Jones Beach, about an hour drive. I remember now, several years removed from the actual day of our meeting, how much I was impressed with Seaman Bovill. It was not a junior/ senior relation we had. We just shared parts of our lives with each other. I remember feeling the sense of a very welcoming person. A smile may be the strongest element of the welcoming personality. I remember clearly his general disposition of being very welcoming, very positive.

I could see he was an individual who had service before self in mind. It's an easy concept to talk about but to really display it, live it, to portray where folks say, "Man, this person really gets it! He's joining a noble service for a noble cause." He shared his upbringing, how he got to where he was. I was very impressed. I had the feeling this person is going to go far in the Coast Guard. He's here for the right reasons. He would have an enduring impact on his workplace. There are individuals within the base who have great influences. I knew that station [Eaton's Neck] would be a good spot with Seaman Bovill there.

Two months after Michael died, Admiral Vojvodich called Michael's parents and asked if he could visit them. He drove on a Sunday from Washington, D.C. (where he was stationed) to the Bovill's home in northern New Jersey. "There is a family feel to the Coast Guard," he said.

Admiral Vojvodich felt that Michael was an integral member of the Coast Guard family:

That element of the family doesn't just stop at the lifelines. We remember the enduring impact family has on us. Michael's influence on me and his shipmates came from his family. The values of his family and the Coast Guard were concentric. Michael had a value set that coincided with the organizational side. Part of it is to save lives. Part of it is to serve before self. His sense of honor, respect, and duty were very obvious to me. Those qualities jumped off Michael.

ROXANNE WATSON

RECIPIENT OF MICHAEL'S HEART

"It is only with the heart that one can see rightly; what is essential is invisible to the eye."

—ANTOINE DE SAINT-EXUPERY,
THE LITTLE PRINCE

Roxanne Watson's first trip after receiving what had been Michael Bovill's heart was to the power tool department of Home Depot located in Nanuet, New York. It was an unfamiliar place for her. "Every day, I went to the power tool section," she said. "I didn't know why I was doing it. The staff at Home Depot knew my story. I'd just stand there for a while. Never bought anything. Up to this point in my life, I had no interest or experience with power tools." Eleven months after receiving Michael's heart, during a live recording of *Oprah*, Roxanne met Michael's family and learned that he had been training to become a helicopter mechanic. He was also a firefighter and, with his father, built his family's home. "Michael had tools in his hands every single day," Roxanne said. Michael's passion was now hers.

For seventy-eight days prior to the transplant, Roxanne lay in bed in the cardiac care unit of Montefiore Hospital waiting either to die or receive a heart. Her weight, normally one hundred fifty pounds, was down to ninety-five. She was unable to walk due to weakness caused by congestive heart failure. Because of the severity of her condition, Roxanne was listed in the highest priority category of the national registry of those needing a heart transplant.

During her hospitalization, she had been alerted three times that a match was imminent. The first heart turned out to be defective. The second went to the person listed as number one in the critical category. Roxanne was number two. The donor of the third heart was a prison inmate at risk for HIV. Roxanne said, "I'd gone through enough. I wasn't going to accept a heart that might make me sick. I refused it. The ups and downs of this process were huge. For me, I knew I wasn't going to die. But for my friends and family, this process was very difficult."

The transplant coordinator who communicated with potential recipients was an observant Jewish woman who did not engage in her job from late Friday afternoon through sunset of Saturday in observance of her Sabbath. "When I got a call from her late on Friday afternoon, I knew that it was serious. I said to her, 'It's almost your Sabbath.' She said to me, 'I wouldn't do this for anyone but you.' That's when I knew it was going to happen."

Roxanne carries a photograph of Michael everywhere she goes. "I've carried this picture every day since I got it. Every single place I go, he goes with me. Michael was in the Coast Guard, twenty-three years old. He saved five of us," she said. "When I met Michael's family on *Oprah*, they gave me this photo. Michael was an awesome kid. He was a fireman, an EMT, and training to be a helicopter mechanic. He just had an accident. He wanted to be a donor. His family knew he wanted to be a donor. He had registered as a donor in New York, New Jersey, and with the Coast Guard. It's bitter. It's sweet. But he saved five of us."

Roxanne has met three of the other recipients of Michael's organs:

I didn't meet the little Spanish girl. She was seven and she received one of Michael's kidneys, but I did meet Elijah, a black kid who received the other kidney. He was eighteen years old and a student at Bronx Community College. A sixty-two-year-old Chinese man, Zhou, got his liver. I think Zhou went back to work. Scott, a thirty-one-year-old Jewish man who had cystic fibrosis, received both of Michael's lungs. Before the transplant, Scott wanted to have children but didn't because of his illness. He didn't think he was going to live long. Now, Scott is a father of two children. I was fifty-six. Michael saved us, people of all ages, colors, religions.

Before her illness, Roxanne was the manager of the TJ Maxx outlet in the Bronx. One day at work she felt she had pulled a muscle.

I went into my office, took some aspirin, and felt better. Then I drove home. For six weeks I went back and forth to work and had this annoying pain. Finally, I went to Nyack Hospital. The doctor in the ER told me I hadn't pulled a muscle. I'd had a heart attack. I went into cardiac care for two years. Things weren't getting better and my name was placed on the list to receive a transplant.

Initially, Roxanne was placed in a category of lesser priority, but as time passed and her condition worsened, her name was placed in the highest priority list. "Then I started dropping five or six pounds a week. I went for a check-up at the hospital. My doctor said, 'You have to stay.' There I lay for seventy-eight days."

Despite being in the hospital for so long, Roxanne never lost hope she might receive the heart she needed:

I never thought I was going to die. I felt I had more living to do. Even when I was at my sickest, when I couldn't walk, I never thought I was going to die. I always felt that something was going to happen and I'd be able to live. And I told my nurses in the hospital that I'd live and I'd save other people's lives by signing up organ donors. I was going to fight and fight and fight and live and I was going to save other people's lives. I was in a lot of pain but I wasn't unhappy.

I had two near-death experiences when I was in the hospital. I'm not afraid to die. Because if dying is like those experiences, it was absolutely no pain. I knew I was going. I saw darkness. I felt a curtain coming across my face. I could actually see it getting darker. I heard my nurse talking to me. She said, "Roxanne, come on. Hold on. Come on back!" I felt she was shaking me. Then I heard them calling a code. I felt motion in the room. I went up to the ceiling and looked down and saw myself in the bed. I saw them working on me. I saw all my doctors. I saw my son. And when I woke up, my doctors weren't there. My son wasn't there. But my nurse was still there. I told her exactly what everyone had said and she was like ... [laughs] "Yes!" I had absolutely no pain at all. It was kind of euphoric. So if that's what happens, I'm not afraid.

True to her word, even while she was bedridden in the hospital, Roxanne began signing people up for organ donation. "To date, I've signed up the most people of anyone in the United States. I've signed up almost ten thousand people. Very proud of that."

Before her illness, Roxanne worked in retail for thirty years:

I worked seventy, eighty hours a week. I loved it, every minute of it. I had been a district manager, but my heart was in the store. I liked dealing with the customers. I wanted the tough store. So I got the store in the Bronx. I'm still close with the folks who worked with me. When I was sick and in Montefiore, my associates from work visited me every day. My family lived in Rockland and it was hard for them to come to the Bronx to visit me.

Roxanne often refers to Michael as "my donor:"

Michael was a baby. He was only twenty-three years old. He went home every Sunday. When he had his accident, he had just left his family in New Jersey. He was in the Coast Guard and stationed on Long Island. His family lived out on Route 78 in New Jersey. He didn't even have a girlfriend yet. Always wanted to be a fireman. He was a volunteer fireman. He wanted to be New York City fireman. He was on the list to become one but he didn't want to wait anymore so he went into the Coast Guard where he was a fireman and training to be a helicopter mechanic. His mother told me that when Michael was a little boy, he'd looked out the window because the fire station was close by and he waited for the firetrucks to go by. He called them "rucks.' He'd go, "Ruck, 'ruck, 'ruck, Mommy!' Every single person we talk to who knew him—his commander, the other people in the Coast Guard, and everybody in his town—they all say, 'Good kid.'"

Roxanne met Michael's mother, father, and three sisters during an episode of Oprah.

Oprah's people asked me to tell my story, Michael's story, and about how I was signing people up for organ donations. The audience already knew that Michael's family was there. I was the only one who didn't. During the show, Dr. Oz, who was one of the guests on the show, gave me the picture of Michael and I just knew it was my donor. That's when the crying started. Then he said, "We have another surprise for you." The studio *door opens and in walks the family. That's when everybody lost it. They had to go to break because everybody was crying. Dr. Oz, the other guests, all the people on stage, everyone in the audience, we were all crying.*

After the break, Roxanne talked about what she was doing since the transplant, which included a major re-decorating of her home. This is when she learned about Michael's lifelong connection to tools and construction.

"Michael's mom says she lost one child and gained five," Roxanne said. "They're really positive about the whole thing. They're deeply Christian. They believe this is the way it was meant to be. Michael's mother lost her son and was upset because they didn't tell her that he could save someone with his eyes. That's the kind of people they are. They just want to help people."

Roxanne spends most of her time now to spreading her message about the importance and significance of becoming an organ donor:

My illness was the best thing that ever happened to me. It put everything in perspective. I've had a fabulous life, both pre- and post-transplant. The post-transplant has been amazing. The things I've been able to do because of Michael. The exposure. The people I'm able to reach. Thousands of people on Facebook. Thousands of people on Twitter. People from all around the world. Because of the story, the purpose that I have. I love Oprah. She says, "When you find your purpose in life, your life becomes easy." Living is easy for me now. I tell the story. For radio, TV, whatever. I do it because I know there's going to be at least one person who's going to listen. And if that one person signs up, they can save five or ten people. It makes it very easy for me to do.

I'm going to donate my whole body to Einstein Medical Center so the kids [the medical students] can play with me [laughs]. That's how I can help somebody else when I pass away. I don't want to suffer. The suffering is hardest on the people closest to you. I don't want to hang around for their sake. When my time is up, I think I would accept it and then I can help somebody in medical school.

One of the almost ten thousand people Roxanne signed up to be organ donors was her best friend. He visited her every day while she was a patient at Montefiore. "He just died," she said.

And he saved seven people. He was forty-four. Had a heart condition. His mother asked me to speak at his funeral. I talked about how he and I laughed and joked about how many people we'd save when we die. And people signed up at his funeral. There was a line waiting to sign up to be donors. I said, "In lieu of flowers, sign up to be a donor." It's stupid, somebody dies, you buy flowers that get thrown away. These people decided they wanted to be like my friend.

A student at Rockland Community College (RCC) was another donor signed up by Roxanne. "He graduated last June and passed away last week," she said. "He used to come by the donor table when I was signing people up at RCC and act like he didn't know me. We knew each other well. He comes up and says, 'I'd like to sign up to be an organ donor,' and we'd laugh. I don't know yet how many people he saved."

Roxanne's schedule is filled with work dedicated to encouraging people to become donors. "This week—street fair in Suffern," she said.

Next week—street fair in Congers. Last week I was invited to Florida to speak to a convention of cardiologists. A conference organizer said, "We need you to talk to the doctors because too often they forget about the patients." I said, "Absolutely." They sent me a ticket the next day and I went. I told the doctors, "Don't forget about the people in the bed." Whatever opportunity I get, I take it.

I think someone wants me to be here. I don't know who or what it is. I don't know if it's God. I don't ask that part. I just know what I have to do. My job is to save lives. Just like how Michael saved mine. He saved mine for a reason. His mother says that all the time. My job is to make sure if people can help each other and save each other that they do. My job is to be a life saver. No doubt about it.

If you are interested in becoming an organ donor, Roxanne invites you to contact her at rxwatson@hotmail.com.

ROXANNE WATSON'S SON

Thirteen days after Kellen Wingate's mother received a heart transplant, he signed her out of the hospital. While reading and signing the release form, Kellen realized his life was dramatically changing. At the time, Kellen was twenty-eight years old. His mother, Roxanne Watson, was fifty-six. "It's different when you're officially labeled something," he said with a laugh.

Kellen felt the daunting pressure of the new responsibility he had in caring for his mother:

She was getting ready to leave the hospital and I was signing the paperwork saying my mother is my responsibility now. It's one thing when you're doing it because you care for this person. But signing the paperwork that says if she passes away, the decision is on you. What happens to her is on you. The realization that you have the medical say-so on her life. You're used to it being the other way around. The parent takes care of you. But now it's one hundred percent you take care of your parent. It makes you really, really, really grown up when you have someone to take care of. It's like when a person has their first child. The person who's been taking care of you for your whole life is one hundred percent relying on you now.

Kellen was born in Wilmington, Delaware. Roxanne was twenty-seven. The relationship between his parents didn't work out and Roxanne and Kellen moved to Spring Valley, New York to be close to her family. Kellen was one year old. He has no siblings.

"She had an itch for retail which involves strenuous long hours," Kellen said.

My father lived in Virginia and my mother and grandmother were dual-raising me in Spring Valley. When my mother was at work—she was working seventy-five to eighty hours a week— my grandmother took care of me. Even if you're a little kid, you see it was tough for her. When you're in retail and you don't have experience, you start at the bottom. You're stocking shelves. You're not even at the register yet. She was working non-stop to make sure I had a roof over my head.

My grandmother had five children. She called my mother "the energetic one." If my mother wanted to be a painter, she would just go and do it. My grandmother said my mother was always looking for something to do. She always wanted to experience new things—a big-time doer.

Fueled by her seemingly limitless energy, Roxanne worked her way up in retail eventually being promoted to store manager. "She was the team leader," Kellen said. "She was selfless—always putting somebody else in front of her." He recalled an example that occurred his senior year in high school:

She took me and her whole overnight crew on vacation to Las Vegas for a week. Her crew was from a very low-income area in the

Bronx. Before this trip, half of them had never left New York City in their entire lives. They were thirty to forty years old. Their store was number one in sales that year and my mother took her Christmas bonus and put that towards the trip. She paid for me and six overnight crew, all on her tab from the bonus she got for their hard work. Spent every dime of the bonus to take me and them on vacation. These are the people who are setting the store up while the day workers are at home asleep. They didn't interact with the day people. Aside from the night manager, the only other person they saw was my mother who would go overnight once or twice a week. She was the one to tell them that they're doing a good job because otherwise, they'd be by themselves.

Myself, I'm an eighteen-year-old and I'd been on five or six vacations leading up to this and I'm talking to a forty-year-old person who never, never left New York City. Now you're talking about getting on a plane, going to the opposite end of the country. It was really something to see an adult human being on vacation for their first time ever. On the trip, I saw that for most of the staff, this was the first time that their presence and good work was appreciated. My mom was putting them on notice that they were appreciated. When you're a leader, you have to find things to get your team going. Everyone has a different motivation and what works for one person might not work on another. She pulls out the good in every person.

Roxanne's health began to decline in 2006. Kellen was twenty-six. At the time, he lived near his mother but in his own home. Kellen was experienced with illnesses in his family. Roxanne's mother suffered three heart attacks and three strokes. "You wouldn't be able to tell," he said.

Kellen described his grandmother's strong nature:

She just kept going. She walked through it. I watched her have two of her heart attacks. Her having a heart attack was like me coming down with a cold. She was a nurse. While she's having the heart attack, she's completely calm, completely poised. She knew what to do. She told me to turn the fan on, get her a drink of water, call 911, tell them the medicines she's taking. It was amazing to see that. That was my vision of someone being sick. So, when my mother got sick, I thought, 'Oh, she's gonna be fine. She's the bolt of lightning. Nothing can take her down.'

Kellen watched and supported Roxanne for the next four years of her decline:

The first few years were really frustrating because there was a series of misdiagnoses. It started with her having severe back pain so that doctor said, "We'll do x, y, and z and it'll be fixed." She didn't get better. Then it went to stomach pain. Then they thought it was something wrong with her ovaries so she got a hysterectomy. Wasn't that. Then they said, "You have Crohn's disease." So, she got surgery for Crohn's disease. Then her ankles and feet were swelling. The doctor said, "Must be something with your circulation." So, they worked on her legs. Then she went to a podiatrist. I kid you not, but he looked at her feet and said, "Something is wrong with your heart." Just like that. This was two years into her decline and this was the first time I was hearing about a problem with her heart.

Kellen took Roxanne to Montefiore Hospital where tests revealed serious cardiac problems.

Throughout the two years, multiple and incorrect diagnoses, Kellen claims he did not feel angry:

I felt super frustrated. I wouldn't say angry. It was upsetting. When you're going back and forth to hospitals for tests and appointments, you start to see how a misdiagnosis in the medical field can be disastrous. You're getting treated for one thing and something else is killing you and you have no idea. I was her primary care giver and still am to this day. When we got the correct diagnosis, it was a relief."

He reconsidered his previous statement regarding not feeling anger:

The only thing that angered me was when we went to a couple of doctors who said, "Nothing is wrong with you. It's in your head. You're fine." That really bothered me. There's no human being who likes to go to the doctor all the time. No one wants to hang out at the doctor's office time in and time out. So, to have a doctor tell her, "There's nothing wrong with you" when there clearly was—well, something is wrong because they could see she'd been to multiple doctors and had multiple diagnoses and procedures and she was still feeling bad. I'm a forgiving person. I have no choice but to be. Just keep moving forward. My father was a person who was really good about getting over stuff. Whatever it was, he was "Get over it! You can avoid it in the future but there's nothing you can about what's already happened." That's how I took it. Makes life much easier.

With the correct diagnosis of congestive heart disease, Roxanne was under the care of her cardiologist, Dr. Julia Shin. In late 2009, Roxanne and Kellen met with Dr. Shin in the doctor's office. "Dr. Shin says to my mother, 'You're going to need a heart transplant,' and I go, 'So, how does that work?'" he said with a laugh. "You just don't understand the process at first. Then I realize that a heart transplant requires someone else dying . . . you know? I don't want that to happen. But, at the same time, you don't want your mother to die. You're stuck in the middle. Somebody else is going to have experience loss for you to gain."

As an inpatient at Montefiore Hospital, Roxanne waited seventy-eight days for the right heart. During that time, three hearts were considered for transplant but turned down for a number of reasons. Kellen was a faithful visitor making the commute from Spring Valley to the Bronx frequently. Then Roxanne's transplant coordinator called him at work:

She told me, "We got a heart and all the preliminary tests say this is going to be the one." It was a one-hundred-minute drive to get to Montefiore from my job. I started work at seven thirty in the morning and got the call about eight fifteen. I told my staff, "I gotta go," and hightailed it to the city as quickly as possible. When I got into the room, I saw there were a lot more doctors there than the last three times. A lot of people running back and forth. There was a greater sense of urgency than before. Then Dr. D'Alessandro [Roxanne's cardiovascular surgeon] comes in. With the first three hearts [that weren't transplanted] he didn't come in. He walks in and says, "It's game time!" and gives two thumbs up. I go with her as she's wheeled into the surgical floor. It's our first time there. I'm holding her hand. She's cracking jokes. Making fun. Right before she's going into the surgical suite, one of Dr. D'Alessandro's assistants gives me her glasses and tells me, "Go kiss your mother before she goes in!" I kiss her and she says, "I'll see you when I'm done."

The waiting room is very nerve-wracking. There's a TV screen that has the name of the patients in surgery, what time their surgery started, the stage they're in. It looks like the arrival screen at airports. You see all these names go up and then the names disappear when they're done. The process starts about three in the afternoon. My uncle, her brother, is with me. We're looking at the screen. When it starts, her name is at the bottom and it slowly goes up. About eight o'clock at night, her name is sitting at the top. About two thirty in the morning, her name is the only one on the screen, and then it goes off. We're wondering, "What does that mean? Is she done?" Rachel, her heart transplant coordinator, comes out at three in the morning. She's crying and smiling and says, "It's all done." Then everyone who was in the operating room comes into the waiting room.

Dr. D'Alessandro, all his assistants, all the nurses—everyone is crying. I remember that one of Dr. D'Alessandro's sleeves still has blood on it. He says, "It's done. The heart went in perfectly." He's crying. He says, "Your mother is the greatest."

About five in the morning, Kellen and his uncle went into in the recovery room. Roxanne's eyelids were taped. She was still asleep. Kellen reported that the nurses caring for his mother were all crying. She had been in the hospital for so long that the staff knew her well. When he looked at Roxanne lying in the recovery room, he thought to himself, *This is your mother and you don't know how this is going to work. The heart she was born with is not there and she's got somebody else's heart. So . . . is she going to act the same? Is she going to be different? What am I receiving?*

The initial answers to Kellen's questions began to reveal themselves the next day when he returned to the hospital. Roxanne was asleep when he arrived. After she woke, Kellen asked her, "Hey! How you doing?" He recalled her responding brightly, "Fine!" That day Roxanne walked with assistance.

Thirteen days after her transplant, Dr. Shin spoke to Roxanne. (During the long hospital wait for a suitable heart, Dr. Shin had become so attached to Roxanne that she told her colleagues if she died that she wanted her heart given to Roxanne.) "Dr. Shin said, 'I'm done with you. Get out of here! You're ready!'" Kellen recalled more about that day:

They give you a book that is full of precautions. I say the title of this book should be You Can't Do Anything! *And it was a big book. Pretty much, this book tells you to go home and sit down and don't do nothing until everything heals. We're looking at the book. It says "Don't do this. Don't do this. You can't eat this." It gives you a tutorial about her medicines. That was outrageous! She was supposed to take almost fifty pills a day for the first six months she was home. Now, all of a sudden, I'm a pseudo-doctor. I remember going home and googling all the medicines to find out what each does so I didn't screw things up. It was a shock for me going from her not being here [at home] to her being here with all these precautions of what she couldn't do. She had to wear a mask when she went out. She couldn't be around small children because their immune systems are still developing and her immune system was on the reset button. She couldn't be out in the sun. She can't have grapefruit ever again in her life. She used to love grapefruit and now can't have it at all. It has a negative reaction with her anti-rejection medicine. I eat grapefruit and I make sure it goes nowhere near her. I had to get used to all these caution flags around her.*

Kellen, who had moved into his own place when he was twenty-six, moved back in his mother when he was twenty-eight:

Once you realize the severity of it [his mother's condition] and she was living on her own. . . there really was no choice. You're not going to leave your ailing mother to deal with it by herself. It was real clear that the right thing was to move back in with her. Absolutely.

It was tough at first. When she first gets home, you have this book that says she can't do anything and I have to do everything for her. As she started getting better and better and better, she decided that the only thing she really wanted to do was raise awareness about what she went through so nobody has to wait one hundred-some days for a heart like she did. She wanted to get out there to make others aware that there are people waiting and dying [needing an organ].

Kellen has been and continues to be Roxanne's primary caregiver. He also works professionally as a personal trainer and actor.

He's appeared on network television programs including *Saturday Night Live, Law and Order,* and *Elementary.* He's also appeared in *Luke Cage, Daredevil,* and *The Defenders* which are spinoffs of the Marvel comic book series produced by Netflix. Typically, he plays detectives, police officers, security guards, and gang members. Kellen, who stands six feet, four inches tall and weighs two hundred fifty pounds, gets those roles because of his size. "I stick out," he said with a laugh. "Being an extra, you're supposed to fill the scene up without taking away from the main character but because of my size, they don't have a lot of choice. I just can't hide in the background."

Explaining how he juggles his jobs and his mother's care, he said, "The good thing about the acting, it's not every day. There are days when I'm home and not at the gym."

Kellen said his mother's experience has influenced his own outlook on life:

> *I've completely changed through this whole process. Now, I don't let little things bother me. They used to. It used to be if it didn't go the way I wanted it to go, it bothered me. Seeing her go through the process. Seeing her hit the reset button. Whatever you're going through, there's always somebody else who's got it much worse than you. You can get through what you need to and tomorrow, if you wake up, you can hit the reset button to move past what you went through yesterday.*

Where his mother survived and thrived a lengthy ordeal, Kellen's father, Bruce Arnold Wingate, died suddenly at the age of sixty-three. Kellen was thirty-two when his father passed away. "My father was healthy Wednesday and dead by Tuesday. Six days. It was out of nowhere. It reminded you of how precious life is. Your health goes, doesn't matter what else you have."

Another change that Kellen sees in himself is his expression of kindness. "I was always aware of opportunities to be kind and sometimes didn't do it," he said. "Now, when I see the opportunity, I say to myself, 'Let me do what I can do . . . if I'm walking through a doorway and I see a woman who's struggling behind me—even if she's ten steps away—I'm holding the door open for her. I make the physical effort for me to take advantage of that opportunity."

Recently, Kellen and Roxanne attended a ceremony honoring Michael Bovill and recognizing Roxanne's astounding success in signing up almost ten thousand organ donors. Michael's mother Jilayne, his sister Mandy, Mandy's husband, and their three children attended, as did Scott Taffet (the recipient of Michael's lungs) and his wife, Stacy. For several minutes this group of nine people—who did not fit the traditional picture of "family" (they are black, white, Christian and Jewish)—stood in a close circle admiring photographs of Scott and Stacy's young children, engaging Mandy's kids, and listening to Kellen's experience as a cast member on *Saturday Night Live* (which took place the night before the event). Aside from the superficial demographic differences, they demonstrated the dynamic of an engaged, connected, loving family. "I had the feeling of family with the Bovills the second we met them six years ago," he said.

Kellen explained how he has unexpectedly gained more family members through this experience:

> *The family connection doesn't happen unless it comes from their side because they're the ones who lost their twenty-three-year-old son and brother, a good man who was on earth trying to make it better. He was serving our country and working as a firefighter. All the great things this man brought to this planet— it doesn't happen unless they raised him the way they did and it doesn't happen unless they were available to be reached out to. There are times when organ recipients reach out to donor families and the donor families don't respond because they just can't deal*

with the loss of their loved one. For the Bovills to bury their child and realize he wanted to donate his organs and for them to make that happen, it takes very special people. And they welcomed us. They do everything they can because their son is spread out among five new people now. They're 1000 percent willing to reach out to us. So, now, I'm not an only child anymore. I've got three sisters. There's no doubt that the family thing was there from day one. There's this constant effort to reach out to each other. The amazing strength they show—it's very contagious.

DR. JULIA SHIN

ROXANNE WATSON'S CARDIOLOGIST

I thought a lot about miracles as I researched Michael and his legacy. A quote from Albert Einstein resonated with me: "There are two ways of looking at the world. One is as though nothing is a miracle. The second is as though everything is a miracle." While I'm uncomfortable with his either/or approach, I lean heavily towards "everything is a miracle." The more I learned, the more miraculous it became to me—recovering Michael's heart, lungs, liver, and kidneys and transplanting them into five other people who would have died without this "miracle." I wondered how the doctors who had intimate connections with Michael's organs experienced this. Did they maintain a clinical detachment, or did they live in a state of awe? Or did they experience some of each? I was eager to speak with them and hear their stories . . .

As a cardiologist, Julia Shin has found herself in remarkably close contact with hundreds of patients (including Roxanne Watson) awaiting heart transplants:

I feel very responsible for my patients. Out of self-preservation instincts, I tend to keep an emotional and professional distance. Otherwise, it would be too mentally exhausting to get too involved with everyone. Roxanne is an exception. I've gotten quite close to her. When Roxanne was waiting for a heart, I knew that our blood types were compatible. I told my colleagues that if I died, I would want my heart donated to Roxanne.

I knew I'd be a doctor when I was a child . . . I don't come from a family of doctors. I come from a Korean family. Stereotypically, we're pushed to be doctors or lawyers.

I was born in Chicago. My parents are from Korea. My dad is South Korean and my mother is North Korean. Her family escaped to the south during the war. They both grew up in poverty and immigrated separately to the U.S. to pursue a higher education. They met in Chicago where my father was studying for his PhD. in chemical engineering and my mother was working. I have one other sibling, a sister, who is a state appellate court judge in Massachusetts. A doctor and a lawyer! My parents fulfilled their American dream.

In addition to cultural and parental encouragement, Dr. Shin possessed a natural inclination towards anatomy, physiology, and medical interventions. "My dad recalls finding me at the age of ten dissecting dead lizards I found in the backyard," she said. "I was fascinated by the internal organs. He also remembers me as a child with a straw trying to do CPR with a dead lizard." She admitted the lizard did not revive , but that didn't squash her aspiration to become a doctor. She knew she had strengths that would help her in attaining her dream:

I was always good with my hands. I played the piano—another traditional Korean thing to do—and I wanted to do something that was procedural. To me, that means using my hands. As a cardiologist, I perform heart biopsies, coronary angiograms, and cardiac catheterizations. Cardiology, aside from surgery, is probably the most technical of the internal medicine specialties. Not to be overly romantic about it, the heart, for me, has a symbolic importance. And the heart and cardiovascular system are very interesting to me. It's the perpetual nature of the heart. We have no control over how the heart beats, how it functions. When I was pregnant, my son's heartbeat was the first sign of life. There is something signifying life that the heart has that the other organs don't.

Within the world of cardiologists, there are surgeons and medical physicians. Dr. Shin decided not to become a surgeon. "I was warned about the time commitment it took to be a surgeon. So, of course, I chose the most time-consuming specialty in internal medicine—and probably work just as hard as a surgeon does. Internal medicine is a bit friendlier towards women if you want to have a family." She is now the mother of two-and-a-half-year-old Dylan Shin.

"Since I've become a mother, my perspective has changed. My son is magical to me. Before him I did not believe in magic. It surprised me very much," she said.

Dr. Shin recalled another experience which evoked a sense of magic. "It was when I was in medical school, seeing my first childbirth—a C-section. I remember seeing the little head pop out of the skin incision and almost fainting from sheer awe."

Her openness to magic may reveal itself in the personal connections she and her patients develop with each other. "I remember Roxanne very well. I remember all the transplant patients," she said.

We form very close relationships with transplant patients. The sheer number of visits we have. I probably met with Roxanne on a bi-weekly basis pre-transplant and then the first year after the transplant at least a dozen times. And after the first year, four times a year. That continues for the rest of the patient's life. I tell them they're marrying us. We're treating them for chronic immunosuppression which can lead to a lot of potential complications down the road. We screen very heavily for coronary disease. We follow their lab work closely with a particular focus on kidney function. Heart transplant patients take immunosuppressive drugs for the rest of their lives.

Roxanne was very special. She has been the most vocal advocate for signing up new donors. It's become her focus. She has a lot of energy. I remember her pre-transplant, her outlook. There are patients we know are going to do well. And there are patients we know are not going to do well. She was one of those patients, even pre-transplant, whose outlook on life was so positive. I knew that barring any tragic occurrences, she would do well. She waited for months in the ICU for a transplant. I don't ever recall her complaining. Not once. She was always smiling. She was always playing Celine Dion music.

When Dr. Shin was alerted that a heart (at that moment still beating in the chest of Michael Bovill) might be available for Roxanne, Dr. Shin or one of her colleagues (Dr. Shin does not remember) began a rigorous screening process to determine if this would be a good match. "At this point, the donor is considered brain dead and is being kept alive with artificial means. It's amazing to take a donor's heart and replace it with someone else's heart. It just keeps going," she said.

Dr. Shin explained how the process works:

Typically we get a call from the coordinator at the donor agency telling us there's an organ available. We go through the history of the donor. Make sure there aren't any red flags for cardiac disease.

I see test results. I don't physically see the actual heart before the transplant. I do see the heart through an echocardiogram which is an ultrasound picture of the heart to make sure the function is fine. We look at the EKG which tests the electrical activity of the heart. And, if indicated, we look at the coronary angiogram to look at the arteries that supply the heart muscle. If everything looks fine for a close match to the recipient, we say, "Yes."

With the signal to proceed from the doctors, the coordinator from the transplant agency (in Michael's case, this was LiveOnNY) takes over. The coordinator informs the patient that they're getting the heart. If the patient is out of the hospital, the coordinator gives them instructions for coming in. Recovery (referred to as "procurement") teams mobilize. In Michael's case there were four separate teams to recover his heart, lungs, kidneys, and liver. Dr. Shin had no direct role in the actual recovery or transplant process.

As part of her training to become a transplant cardiologist, Dr. Shin observed an actual transplant:

I went on a donor run with the procurement team. It's not just the heart team. It's the lung team, the liver team, the kidney team. They quite literally descend on this donor like vultures. In the end—and this is the part that I always remember—the donor torso is completely empty. It looked like the ribs of a canoe. The ribs of the donor look like the concave ribs of a canoe. The feeling was like when you hear certain musical phrases that do that to me—your hair will stand up and you feel that shiver down your back. It's not a common sensation.

Being a doctor, I've seen that life and death is a process of nature. Before I had my son, it was much more of an objective occurrence. As a doctor, I deal with death all the time. I never feared death even though I see it all the time. It's just the way life is. The way the universe is. I remember reading about how

incomprehensibly enormous the universe is. We are just a fleeting,
miniscule moment in the universe. That to me is very comforting.
If I die, I was never that significant in the scope of things.

Dr. Shin's picture of the immensity of the universe, the immensity of time and how it comforts her began to live in me. It gave me perspective about the importance—and lack of importance—of what I felt. Both good and bad feelings became more of a momentary experience that I could choose to hold on to or let go of. Dr. Shin's picture helped me to let go of my "fleeting, miniscule moment in the universe" and freed me to be able to enter each moment with a freedom to be more fully present in this moment.

In planning for her own death, Dr. Shin is signed up to be an organ donor. "There's a woman who is listed [awaiting transplant] right now who is my blood type. If I were to donate my heart to someone, it would mean more to me to donate to someone that I know, who I've taken care of, and that she would benefit from it."

Talking about Roxanne specifically, Dr. Shin said, "I've been a cardiologist for eleven years, not including the training. It can get much routinized after a while. Every so often there is a patient like Roxanne who makes me and my colleagues recognize that this is why we do what we do. That we have saved her life so that she can save all the lives she has."

ROXANNE WATSON'S CARDIOVASCULAR SURGEON

D r. David D'Alessandro does stuff that strikes me as miraculous. He is the surgeon who took in his gloved hands the heart that beat in the chest of Michael Bovill and successfully transplanted it into the chest of Roxanne Watson. And just before he accomplished this remarkable feat, he had surgically removed Roxanne's original and diseased heart from her body and initiated mechanical life support that enabled her to survive temporarily *with no heart!*

I've seen enough movies and television shows where surgeons operate on another level from the rest of us mere mortals. I anticipated a type-A personality on steroids.

To talk to this rock star of medicine, I screwed on my conviction to set aside any inclination to be intimidated.

Before the actual interview, Dr. D'Alessandro's administrative assistant fielded my phone calls and emails. I forwarded the article that I had written about Roxanne who had confirmed with the doctor that she was comfortable with his speaking to me about her.

With these steps in place, scheduling the interview was relatively easy. Confirming the interview was an open issue. This is a guy whose work life can be any day of the week at any time of the night or day. If he was in the middle of an unscheduled emergency surgical procedure (Are emergencies ever scheduled?), he was not about to do anything other than sew an aorta in place as if someone's life depended on it. *Because someone's life depended on it!* His job as a heart surgeon would supersede an interview with me.

When we exchanged preliminary emails, Dr. D'Alessandro signed his note "Dave." I was surprised. While I expected a more formal "Dr. D'Alessandro," I was pleased—and a bit disarmed—by the ease with which he put us on first-name basis.

When we spoke, Dave was friendly, approachable, professional, and precise. I asked him many questions.

Some were technical. ("What is the order of events when you perform a heart transplant?")

Some were personally anatomical. ("You're in surgery for many continuous hours. What do you do when you have to pee?")

Some were intimate. ("When you perform a heart transplant, do you experience awe, beauty and/or magic?")

Dave answered them all as if I was the only person in the world and this was the only thing he had to do . . .

Dr. David D'Alessandro pauses when asked, "Is the heart the container of the soul?" Dr. D'Alessandro, the surgical director of Heart Transplantation and Mechanical Circulatory Support at Massachusetts General Hospital, responds to technical questions related to the heart and heart transplants—he reports performing "more than one hundred, less than two hundred"—with clarity and precision. He waited until the questions related to procedures and techniques were posed and promptly presented thorough responses. The pause after hearing "Is the heart the container of the soul?" was long.

"My personal belief is that the person is the mind and the brain," he said. He explained further:

The heart, lungs, kidneys, liver, and other organs keep the brain alive. Religiously, I believe in the soul. And where is the soul? I don't know. It used to be thought it resides in the heart, but when I'm transplanting a heart I'm not taking someone else's soul and putting it in someone else. I hope the soul is not in the heart because of what I do [laughs]. Religion and spirituality are not scientific. It's just what you believe. Perhaps a part of the human being is in the liver, another part in the kidneys, another part in the lungs and heart. I don't know. Who am I to say it's not true?

Dr. D'Alessandro's decision to become a surgeon was almost a forgone conclusion. "My grandfather was a surgeon. My father was a surgeon. So, it was a way of life that I grew up with," he said. The family connection but also the sense of personal duty led Dr. D'Alessandro to pursue his current profession:

It was the esteem that people held for my dad. He was respected in the community and he was someone who I looked up to. People respect physicians who dedicate themselves to the wellbeing of their patients. He worked hard. I'd run into patients of his who were very grateful. Those were influential exchanges to me as a young person. I was focused on becoming a physician from early high school years. I never really wavered from it. I went with my dad two or three times to see him operate and scrubbed into the field and watched what he did. As a small kid, I went with him when he did rounds. Mostly that was driving around to different hospitals and sitting in waiting rooms, waiting for him [laughs]. The nurses would walk by and say, "You're Dr. D'Alessandro's son. Your dad is great." It felt good. It felt like something I wanted to do. I knew I wanted to be a physician right after I outgrew wanting to be an astronaut and a fireman and a policeman. That was by seventh or eighth grade. I had thought about being an architect because I like to construct and draw. I like to work with my hands. I sort of like to tinker. Architecture interested me but other than that, I never really seriously dabbled in anything else other than becoming a surgeon.

After graduating from college, Dr. D'Alessandro worked for two years in a research lab where he had his first exposure to heart surgery and the cardio-pulmonary bypass machine. For the next four years, he attended medical school at Columbia University Vagelos College of Physicians and Surgeons. To become a cardiac surgeon, Dr. D'Alessandro trained for five years in general surgery followed by two years of cardio-thoracic surgery. He was thirty-six when his training was complete.

"I think the physiology of heart surgery and the technology that we use to perform operations is exciting and constantly evolving," he said.

It's an area of surgery that is technically and technologically demanding. It's a young field as fields go. It's been around for about only fifty years. The progress that's been made in those fifty years has been tremendous. Operating on a heart is very different from any other organ than I've been exposed to, which is pretty much all of them. Some argue that operating on the brain is technically demanding but surgery on the brain is not very interesting. The brain just kind of sits there. The heart is a beautiful piece of machinery. When you watch it in a diseased state and you're able to intervene to make it better, or in the case of Roxanne, to replace it, it's very transformative.

During his career, how Dr. D'Alessandro experiences his work has changed:

*I can remember the first several times seeing transplant operations
and how exciting it was. Earlier in my career, I was doing a lot
of procurements—that is taking the organs from the donors and
bringing them back for transplant—and watching them being
sewn in and seeing them begin to work. It was so exciting. I can
remember the exhilaration I'd get as a medical student and a
junior resident. I don't feel that excitement anymore. It's become
so routinized that the reward has diminished. To the patients, it
is transformative. Unfortunately for me, doing it day in and day
out, it's not as impactful.*

Typically, Dr. D'Alessandro meets his transplant patients
before the actual surgery. "If they're sick and in the hospital, I see
them more frequently," he said. There have been occasions where
the first time he saw the recipient was on the operating table, but
this is rare. "Occasionally, patients are seen and evaluated by other
surgeons and listed for transplant. In this case, I might only meet
them when they come in for their transplant."

The cardiovascular transplant surgeon is one member of a
multi-disciplinary team, all of whom have a voice in the evaluation
and determination of treatment plans for prospective patients.
Potential transplant patients are ranked on a list based on their
need and health. "Patients can sometimes be listed [designated to
receive an organ] for several years when their symptoms are stale,"
Dr. D'Alessandro said. "As their heart failure progresses, they move
up on the list. When they get to the top tier of the list, typically
they will get transplanted within about six months depending on
their blood type and body size. Or they might get lucky and be
listed for two or three weeks."

He further explained the process:

*We'll get an organ offer—unfortunately it usually wakes you up
in the middle of the night [laughs]. A cardiologist or transplant*

coordinator will call and say, "We have an organ for so and so." We'll get specifics of the donor—cause of death, age, conditions the donor may have (for instance the donor might have been a drug user or alcoholic or diabetic), what the function of the heart is, how well it's working. Then we make the decision whether we'll accept that donor and say, "Yes, we'll take it." If we do say yes, we call our recipient into the hospital and make arrangements to set up the procurement (removal of the organ of the donor). The recipient operation and procurement are usually performed simultaneously because we are keeping the time the organ is out of the body to a minimum.

My role in the transplant process is to help make the decision about the suitability of a particular organ to a particular patient. I perform the transplant operation in concert and close coordination with the procurement team. As a physician, my duties are to care for patients with complex heart disease; to plan and to perform operations when necessary and appropriate; and to see those patients through to successful recoveries.

The coordination between the procurement team and transplant team is crucial to the process. The goal is for the procurement team to arrive with the heart in the operating room where the transplant will be performed as quickly as is safely possible and as close to the time that the transplant recipient's original heart has been removed. "Once we have verification that an organ is suitable for transplant—that is, the procuring surgeon has visualized the organ and told us that it is functioning normally and looks to be a good heart—then we put the patient to sleep on our end and begin the operation," Dr. D'Alessandro said.

Dr. D'Alessandro offered a simplified yet thorough explanation of the process:

We open the chest. It often takes two to three hours to get the recipient's heart out, so we put them on a heart-lung machine (which mechanically supports the function of the patient's heart and lungs). We dissect out the heart and the great vessels and when the procurement team arrives at the local airport—if they're flying in—or if they're nearby and coming by vehicle, we ex-plant [remove] the recipient's diseased heart so that the patient will be without a heart when the donor team walks into the room with the donor organ. We inspect it. We make sure it's not damaged, that there are no holes, or if there's anything that needs to be fixed, and then we'll give it a drink of cardioplegia which is an oxygenated protective solution to the coronary arteries because it's been out of the body for a couple of hours and then we'll sew the heart in.

To connect the heart, there are five connections to be made. You have to reconnect the atrium, the inferior vena cava, the superior vena cava, the pulmonary artery, and the aorta. Although the order can change if you need to, generally the last reconnection is the aorta. Then we take off the aortic clamp to reestablish blood flow. We like to have that done within four hours from the time the donor heart is cross-clamped and removed from the donor to the time that the cross clamp is removed from the recipient. If needed, we can safely exceed the four hours. Once the clamp is off and we reestablish blood flow, the heart will generally start to beat on its own. It will sometimes require a shock but usually starts on its own and beats in a normal rhythm. Then we resuscitate the patient on bypass for a while. This depends on how long the heart has been out and then we wean the patient from bypass which is when we start to oxygenate the patient through their own lungs and then gradually lower the cardio-pulmonary bypass flow until the machine is turned off. Then we pull out the cannulae, the tubes that are connected to the patient that circulate the blood. We reverse the blood thinner with protamine (blood thinners are infused into the patient during surgery). We obtain hemostasis which means that we get all the suture lines to *dry up and stop bleeding. We put in our drainage tubes and then we close the incision and bring the patient back into the ICU for recovery. That process can take three to four hours at its shortest and it can take ten to twelve hours at its longest. That depends on the condition of the recipient.*

The stamina of the head surgeon is critical to a successful transplant. Not only is he or she standing for hours on end but also concentrating and performing fine and gross mechanical tasks; monitoring the wellbeing of the patient; navigating anxiety and tension that must be a part of this life and death process; observing and supervising several colleagues and sometimes performing this operation in the middle of the night, like all human beings, the surgeon may experience the need to urinate.

"There are times during the procedure that you can excuse yourself if you have to," Dr. D'Alessandro said, laughing. Yet he admitted that this isn't a frequent issue:

I can tell you that as a surgeon you almost never have to leave the operating room to urinate [laughs]. I've heard that there's a higher incidence of bladder cancer amongst surgeons than the general public. I'm not sure if that's true. I've never looked it up. It would make sense to me. I think we learn how to hold our urine for a long period of time. But there are times in the course of an operation that I can take a break. That might be if we're ahead of the procurement team and they're not quite there yet, during the resuscitation phase when the patient's still on bypass but the heart is beating and we're waiting for the heart to recover, you can take a few minutes break, or when we're trying to get hemostasis when you're packing suture lines and basically waiting. When you do this work for a long period of time, it seems as if it's sort of second nature. It's not something I dread or even think about. The time goes pretty quickly when you're concentrating. I remember being a medical student, being exhilarated but also shifting my weight back and forth and wondering "When is this thing going to end?" Those long operations when you're watching are much, much longer than when you're doing.

While Dr. D'Alessandro spoke about his work, I was more and more struck by how utterly amazing—to me—this work is. After surgically removing a beating heart from one (brain-dead) person, the "recovered" heart stops beating. The recovery team brings this heart to another patient whose diseased heart has just been removed and is temporarily being kept alive by external "life support" machines. The recently removed heart arrives and is implanted into the patient's chest, the surgical connections are made, and then ... most of the time ... the heart begins to beat on its own. The phrase "doesn't miss a beat" becomes the miracle of life for someone who otherwise would die. I didn't reveal any of my sense of wonder to Dr. D'Alessandro as I asked him about the role of awe, beauty, and magic in his experience as a heart transplant surgeon.

He responded:

We see it every day on routine heart surgery. When this first happened, it was amazing to watch and as a medical student, that's always exciting when you take the clamp off and the heart starts to beat again. If you've never seen it before, that would be an exciting moment for you. Having done it for a long time, the excitement wears off. I sometimes will get dread if the heart doesn't wake up and look good the way I would expect it to. That unfortunately does happen on occasion. I rarely get the exhilaration of the good, but I do feel the dread of the not good. That's the part I feel affects me the most. That's the biggest drawback to what I do. The peaks are not as high as the lows are low. That can affect surgeons who do high-risk operations.

Doing routine heart surgery where we're stopping and starting the heart, it's something we see every day. You deliver cardioplegia (the intentional and temporary cessation of cardiac activity) to the heart to get it to stop, you replace or repair a valve, you do a few by-passes and you take the clamp off and a few minutes later it's beating and acting like you were never there. In most cases it's beating better than before. That's a moment we experience with such routine, it's no longer exciting. The awe and beauty I see is more when you watch a patient who is very, very sick and gets well again. In the case of Roxanne who's so grateful and is empowered to go on and do meaningful things that affect other people's lives, that's where you see that what we do can have such reverberating effects on families and extended families. There are times when we have a patient who is very sick with a heart that we're unsure we can make better and we do something that makes that person get better, there's awe in that. There's so little that we actually know, and yet there's so much we can do with that little bit of knowledge we have. There's a lot to be learned and a lot of discoveries to be made.

Initially, I felt disappointed with Dr. D'Alessandro's response. Where my response to his description was the hair on my neck standing up, his answer felt mechanical to me. I wished that he would live in a state of awe with the miraculous work that I believe he makes manifest. That disappointment dissipated almost immediately, replaced by a different sense of awe. Here is a doctor who must focus one hundred percent of his attention, skill, stamina, and commitment to the wellbeing of the human being whose life is literally in his hands. His insistence on performing the technical/mechanical aspects of his work with impeccable precision was far more essential to the successful gift of life than if the surgeon was mesmerized—during the actual surgery—by anything other than achieving perfection of his or her surgical technique. I recognized that he is committing a selfless act of love for another human being through his work.

From his early childhood through medical school, residency, and career as a surgeon, Dr. D'Alessandro has witnessed many physicians. He recognized that physicians are challenged to perform complex medical assistance while interacting with the patient who is a human being. "Physicians are not all in the same mold. We're no different from people in other professions," he said.

Dr. D'Alessandro went on to explain his ideologies regarding his profession:

There are humanists and there are technicians and everything in between. I've met amazing technicians who I don't feel are good doctors—they don't relate well to patients as people. There are doctors with phenomenal bedside manner who you wouldn't want to operate on you [laughs]. I like to think that we go into the field as physicians because we like to interact with people. And we're human beings who like to improve the lives of others. I like to think that's the motivating factor and everything that comes after is on top of that. Surgery is technically challenging and demanding. When I was operating on Roxanne Watson, I knew who she was but when you're doing the operation, you're not thinking of her as a person—you're doing the technical components of the operation and doing them well. But after the operation, there's no lower feeling than when your patient doesn't do well. Even if you know you did everything right. It's a really sinking feeling. That affects us the most.

I used to do more procurements earlier in my career. They were pretty sterile. You knew the cause of death but there wasn't much else you knew about the donor. And, by and large, we still don't know much. But now, sometimes before the procurement starts, the coordinator on the donor side will read a statement by the family of the donor and request a moment of silence from the surgical teams who are there to take the organs. Those statements can be really emotionally charged. It doesn't make the process any easier. I can tell you that. But it does remind us of what we're doing and the gift that we're taking and passing along to someone else.

I remember Roxanne from her being in the CCU (cardiac care unit) at the hospital waiting for a transplant and I got to know her. But I've come to know her since the transplant because she's been so vocal about the donation process. I have a picture of her with Magic Johnson on my desk here that she gave me.

In addition to his practice as a surgeon, Dr. D'Alessandro is what he calls "an academic surgeon" teaching medical students and trainees:

I don't teach people how to act or how to conduct their duties on a day-to-day basis. It's not necessarily my role. There are many ways to be a successful doctor and physician. The way I do it is by taking good care of patients. Most of all caring. I hope that students will learn by my example. Technically, I teach them in the operating room how to put a stitch in and how to hold the needle, how to contort their body to get the right needle angle, how to manage the heart-lung machine and to a great degree who to operate on and who not to operate on. One lesson I teach is that the enemy is always all around— often disguised as friends. That's to remind people that people make mistakes all the time. As a surgeon, particularly as a heart surgeon, when we're at the center of a complex operation surrounded by people there to assist in the operation and to help manage the patient—that means nurses and perfusionists and anesthesiologists—we are ultimately responsible for everything happening to that patient. We have to always be cognizant and vigilant that when you ask for something, it happens and that *things aren't happening without you being aware of it because mistakes do happen and they happen a lot in complex systems. Surgeons have to be hyper-aware of that. Mostly correct things happen, but that doesn't mean we can let our guard down to not be checking and double-checking all the time. It's something you're doing mentally all the time.*

With the "ultimate responsibility" and monumental consequences of success and failure that may weigh heavily on the surgeon, tension and anxiety can play a significant role in the hours-long transplant process. "If you walked into one of my operating rooms, I don't think you'd experience a lot of tension," Dr. D'Alessandro said. For the most part, he tries to maintain a calm, focused operation room:

There would be times and situations that might get tense but most of the time, it's not going to feel that way. There's often music playing. There's often light discussion that's going on in the background away from the procedure. Inwardly, there's always a degree of tension and anxiety that you have to keep in check. I have no idea what my blood pressure is during surgery [laughs]. I don't want to know. I suspect there are times when it goes up. My pulse, too.

I always have a veto over what music is played. I'll switch it up for others in the room. Classic rock is my mainstay, sometimes we'll listen to more contemporary or country, sometimes classical. I don't like the hip hop too much. It's not conducive to cardiac surgery, in my opinion, so we stay away from that. But I'm pretty broad musically. I get tired of the same thing too much, so we switch it around.

Like all human beings, surgeons age. Physical skills erode. Mental faculties slow down. Given the pressures of their work, surgeons may just wear out. With the responsibilities of a surgeon—

literally being a knife's edge between life and death—the decision of when it's time to hang up the scalpel is critical to the surgeon and his or her patients. "It's a hard thing," Dr. D'Alessandro said.

There are some people who know it's time to quit and there are others who don't. Surgeons often retire but they never really leave. They're still participating in grand rounds and connected, it's hard to break those bonds and they still get emotional enjoyment and intellectual stimulation being involved. I'll know it's time for me to stop when I'm tired. I do feel tired today [laughs]. The last couple of days have been long. Two nights ago we had a transplant. They often go through the course of a night and then you have your day job.

Even though he was feeling the effects of his day job and his night job, Dr. D'Alessandro is still in the thick of operating. Recognizing his experience of the lows directly related to his work, he continues and cited this example of what keeps him going:

There was a young patient who had two transplants. After the second transplant, there were still complications and the patient was in pain. The patient came to see me. It was not a simple issue. I spent a lot of time considering how to fix the condition. Initially, it wasn't obvious I'd be able to help. I sought the advice of other physicians and dragged it on for several months until I was sure that I could do it safely. The last thing I wanted to do is hurt the patient. I just wanted to help. We did the operation. It only took two hours to complete. It was not as hard as I thought it would be. After the surgery, the patient felt much better and gave me the biggest hug. It's moments like that are so rewarding that they make up for all the negative stuff. It was so meaningful to the patient. It felt good to be able to do that. There are times in this field that you can get into the emotional dumps because we're expected to do what we do with outstanding results. There

are no parties when you have outstanding results, but you feel
really lousy when you have something less than that. It feels like
your fault even if you tell yourself it's not. It's just the nature of
taking care of people. It's part of the business. It's part of what
you have to get used to.

He paused and added, "And the hug from my patient helped
me a lot, too."

Dr. D'Alessandro was born into the world of surgeons. He has
devoted much of his life to the work his grandfather and father
did before him. He reflected on his own father's sense of his son's
work and whether he hopes his two children (both boys ages ten
and fourteen) will follow in the D'Alessandro surgical tradition.
"My dad is proud of me," he said with certainty. When it comes to
his sons' future professional aspirations, Dr. D'Alessandro remains
open-minded:

It's a yes/no answer if I'd like my kids to become physicians. The
downside of my job is that I'm always on call to some extent.
There's a lot of times I can't be at places I'd like to be because
of what I do. There's no way I can pass on the care of one of
my patients to somebody else and expect they'll have the same
level of emotional connection that I have. As surgeons, we have
this connection with a patient that never goes away. That's both
special and difficult. So, I would love that one of my boys would
decide to become a doctor because that would mean that they
emulated what I do and, to some degree, proud of what I did.
That would be really meaningful. For my family, it's a tradition
to do that. And I would appreciate that. But if they decided to do
something totally different, it wouldn't bother me. I'm sure that
whatever they do, I'll be proud of that. I would like to know, to
some extent, that they didn't have that burden in their lives that
I sometimes feel is a burden in my life.

With so much of his work involving transplanting hearts, it's important to acknowledge that Dr. D'Alessandro is signed up to be a donor. "I've told Roxanne that she has helped more people [through her prolific signing up of organ donors] with what she does than I help with what I do," he said. "She gets that message out to thousands of people and she's made a real difference. One donor can make a tremendous impact on multiple recipients but also on the families and communities of those recipients. It's part of why I like transplantation. It's amazing what a transplant can do."

SCOTT TAFFET

RECIPIENT OF MICHAEL'S LUNGS

B efore receiving a double lung transplant in 2010, Scott Taffet (then thirty-one years old) wondered if he'd be able to sing better. "Before the transplant, I was a terrible singer," he admitted with a laugh. "I hoped my donor would help me. Apparently, he wasn't a great singer either." Aside from his singing, however, Scott's life dramatically changed for the better after receiving what had been the lungs of Michael Bovill.

Before the transplant, Scott was so short of breath from walking twenty steps from his desk to the copier that he would print multiple files at the same time to minimize the number of trips. Immediately after the transplant, he was thrilled with his ability to breathe well, that his fingers were no longer cold and blue, and that he had color in his face. After a lifetime of experiencing the symptoms of cystic fibrosis (CF)—which include poor growth; poor weight gain despite normal food intake; accumulation of thick, sticky mucus; frequent chest infections; and coughing and shortness of breath—he suddenly faced life without an oxygen cannula inserted in his nose and a huge array of opportunities that had not been possible before.

"Growing up—and to this day—I have cystic fibrosis," Scott said. The disease didn't prevent him from having a normal childhood though:

"As a child and young man, the condition had a limited effect on my life. When I was a boy, I could run and play with other children. I went to school, sleep-away camp, and college with no problem. I had to do treatments but—credit to my parents and credit to myself—I never let it affect me. I had to do physical therapy treatments every morning. I used a nebulizer. I had to watch my weight because cystic fibrosis patients have trouble gaining weight. I took pills but I never let it affect me.

When he was twenty-five, Scott's condition worsened:

It affected me pretty severely. I was on IV therapy, mostly self-administered, sometimes required hospitalization. It took a toll. My exercise tolerance went down significantly. When I was twenty-nine and thirty, it got really bad. I had graduated from law school and was working as a lawyer, but my life was tough. As much as I wanted to be a normal person, not being able to breathe is difficult. Being out of breath after walking from one side of a room to the other is not a good feeling. I was often on oxygen. It was hard on my family. Hard on my wife. I got on the transplant list in November of 2009. I had to go through a series of tests to show that I qualified to be on the list. They administered dozens of tests, everything from lung function—to see how poorly your lungs are doing—to how well your heart is. There were psychological and walking tests. It's a determination to see if you're sick enough to qualify for the list but not too sick that you couldn't have the surgery if there was a matching set of lungs available. My other organs were relatively healthy. I tried to live as full a life as possible. I had a full-time job. I went to work every single day. And it was difficult.

Scott's will is remarkable. Describing his challenges before the transplant, he never said the word "suffers." With his severe symptoms and being on oxygen much of the time, he continued to work full time.

"That's just the way you should do it," he said. "If you can do it, you do it. To sit home and feel sorry for yourself, it was never something I was going to do." He stopped briefly to wipe away tears before continuing:

> It came from my parents. They never treated me as if I was different from others. They said, "This is stuff you have to do," and I did it. I went to school. I went to camp. I went to college. I went to law school. I knew a lot of CF patients whose parents held them back and my parents didn't do that. They were "can do" people. Since becoming a parent, I've learned that it's a lot easier being a patient than a parent.

He paused again as more tears fell. "I can't imagine it was easy for my parents given my condition." Scott needed two new and healthy lungs which, according to him, are hard to come by:

> The lungs are the hardest organs to transplant because they are the biggest and usually sustain the most trauma in accidents. They don't want to give you lungs that aren't going to work well. Sometimes the donor is a smoker. Sometimes there is scarring. Livers, kidneys, and hearts are smaller and more protected and generally survive trauma better than lungs. And I needed two. Some people just need one. So, I needed a donor with two healthy lungs. Even though Michael was in a serious motorcycle accident, his lungs emerged intact.

"After I got on the list, I had two and half 'dry runs,'" Scott said. A "dry run" is when someone on the transplant list is called to the hospital and prepped for surgery. Then the doctors examine the proposed lungs and see if they are a good match. If they aren't, the patient is sent back home to wait . . ."It's a real kick in the gut." Scott described the experience further:

> *For the first five minutes after the dry runs, my sense of humor was pretty bad. I think most recipients go through three dry runs. I knew it was not out of the ordinary. They prep you that this is likely to happen. So I was ready. But you certainly get your hopes up each time. I was going to get my lungs at Columbia Presbyterian Hospital and I was in the city a lot for work. Every time I drove by the hospital, I'd think, "Maybe they'll call now." Didn't happen. It was tough, but I tried to be optimistic.*

His first dry run was in December of 2009. The second was in April 2010. The third (which he refers to as the "half time") was the day before Scott actually received the lungs that had been Michael's. "That's why I call a 'half time,'" he said. He went to the hospital on a Thursday night thinking he would get another set of lungs. He waited all night. "Friday morning they come in and say, 'The lungs are no good.' I'm getting pretty upset. A few minutes later, another doctor comes in and says, 'We may have another set of lungs.' So, I sat in the hospital for the rest of Friday. Friday night they come in and say, 'The lungs are good,' and I was about to have surgery."

"From the time you're told that you've got a good match, you've got about five minutes before they take you to surgery. You have no time to think. It was a blur and I barely remember this part. I remember saying goodbye to my parents and my wife," he said with his voice breaking and stopping to wipe tears away.

> *I never at any time had a fear of dying. It never entered my mind. I had confidence that I was well enough to go through the surgery, confident in the physicians. If you're feeling good,*

it certainly helps. I had that. I remember waking up on Sunday morning. My parents and wife were with me very soon after I woke up. They said, "You look good!" Even though I had tubes coming out me everywhere, there was color in my face. They were used to my face having no color and my hands being blue because of the lack of oxygen. And now I had color! They were happy. Very soon, I felt it was so much easier to breathe despite just having completed major surgery. No changes like suddenly I want to eat ham sandwiches. The difference was that I felt thousands of times better than I did before the transplant. I was out of bed in a couple of days. I was home within ten days. I could move around. It was a world of difference.

Perhaps the greatest change was Scott and his wife, Stacy, decided to have children. "Before the surgery, with my health the way it was, we knew it wasn't the right time. After the surgery, we knew it was the right time," he said. The transplant took place July 16th, 2010. On December 31, 2011, Stacy gave birth to their daughter, Brooke. He was there for her birth. "It was a fantastic moment—one I'll never forget," he said. "Because I'm Jewish, we gave Brooke a Hebrew name. We wanted to name her Michaela after Michael. In Hebrew, the name means 'who is like God?' or 'gift from God.' We asked Michael's parents for their permission and we were so happy that the Bovills were thrilled with it. We were so happy that they were able to be there at the ceremony," Scott said. The Bovills (who are devout Christians) attended Brooke's naming ceremony at the Taffets' synagogue. During the ceremony, Scott said this about Michael:

Brooke's Hebrew name is Michaela and is in memory of Michael Bovill, my lung donor. We can honestly say that without Michael's gift, we would not be standing here today. Stacy and I have had the pleasure of getting to know Michael's beautiful family who are with us today. Through them, we learned that Michael's decision to be an organ donor was in line with the traits he displayed throughout his life. Michael was a firefighter and then a member of the Coast Guard, always wanting to assist those who were in need. Michael was a wonderful son to John and Jilayne and an unbelievable brother to Mandy, Marissa, and Madilyn, and as soon as she can understand, Brooke will know about Michael and his significance to our lives.

Scott's relationship with the Bovills began while he was still in the hospital:

I wrote to thank them. Within a month, they responded. We exchanged letters a couple of times. Then the organ donor people put together a meeting of the recipients with the donor family. We met. It was fantastic. I was so happy to meet them and the other recipients. I was a little nervous before it began. The recipients were put in a room together and we talked for a while. When the Bovills came in everyone applauded. Each of the recipients spoke. I spoke about our plan to have a child. It was really nice to put faces to the names. We kept in touch. A couple months later, my mother, father, wife, and I went out to their house to see the Bovills. They showed a slide show of Michael. It was very touching.

With healthy lungs, Scott took on new missions. "When I was in the hospital, people asked me if there was anything I needed. I told them they could become organ donors. In 2011, I ran a 5K race. In 2013, I ran a 10K. The 10K was connected with the Boomer Esiason Foundation." The foundation encourages people with cystic fibrosis to incorporate exercise into their everyday lives, provides athletes a way to raise money for CF, and offers an avenue for athletic events to contribute to the fight against CF.

The biggest change is that Scott is a father to Brooke, and her younger brother, Aaron. "Life is good and busy. It's great and it's tiring. I wouldn't give it up for anything. My purpose in life now is to be a good father. I think about Michael every day. I have a photograph of Michael on my nightstand. Without Michael and the operation, that wouldn't have been possible."

SCOTT TAFFET'S WIFE

E ven though Stacy Taffet knows she and her husband, Scott Taffet, are two separate human beings, when Scott's lungs were so compromised that he needed transplants, Stacy said, "It was a relief when we got on the list [to receive a lung transplant]." Reflecting on her use of "we" as opposed to "Scott," Stacy said, "It certainly felt like it was my destiny as much as Scott's."

Stacy and Scott met each other in their freshman year at the University of Pennsylvania. They were eighteen years old. Their first meeting was a group dinner shortly after the fall semester began:

> That's where we met. We had a lot of shared interests and always had a good time together. Both of us love musical theater [laughs]. We got together over that shared passion. Over time, I became a huge sports fan. Scott already was. Before me, Scott wasn't a big fan of country music. I was and he became a fan. Both of us played tennis. We're both quite competitive. When we started to date, we'd compete against each other. We made up decathlons. We played tennis and golf and ping-pong and Trivial Pursuit and bowling and all sorts of fun things and competed against each

other. I always won [laughs]. That's not really true. It depended
on the game.

In December of our sophomore year, we decided to commit
to each other. We were nineteen. We both knew it was right and
we'd be crazy not to be together when we knew we were so much
better as a couple. In 2007, we got married. That was eight and
a half years later, but it didn't matter because we knew we were
committed to each other.

When they first met, Scott was in good health. Early in their
relationship, Scott revealed that he had cystic fibrosis, a degenerative
disease of the lungs. "I understood the gravity but he appeared
well," she said. Stacy moved to Boston when she was twenty-five to
attend business school for two years. Scott remained in New York.
It was at that time that Scott's health started to decline:

That was hard because we weren't together all the time. We'd speak
every day and see each other on the weekends. It was clear he
was experiencing challenges [to his health]. I had full information
and knew what it meant that Scott had cystic fibrosis. It was
very hard for me when his health began to deteriorate, but at no
point did I question that we were together. We both tried to stay
optimistic knowing that there were always advances in medicine
and that every day there was something new that could improve
the quality of his life. We thought at some point a transplant
would be on the horizon. We tried to stay optimistic and manage
each challenge as it came. Scott is incredibly positive and that
helped me get through it. I was concerned with how the rest
of our lives would be. We certainly wanted to have a family.
I knew there was a chance that wouldn't happen. But part of me
knew that if we stuck together, we'd get through it one way or
the other. Either something would work out or we'd enjoy every
second we had. When it's right it's right. Some people would have

walked away. *Part of what I love about Scott so much—and why so many people love him—is because of the character that has come out of what he has dealt with. Of course, I'd rather he be completely healthy, but he is who he is because he's had to deal with a lot of challenges. It's what makes him such an incredible, special person. We make each other better [laughs]. We're really a strong team and when I went through challenges, he always helped me get through it. We help each other. We enjoy the good times and get through the hard times. Because of what we've gone through, it makes the smaller obstacles seem less important.*

After graduating from business school, Stacy was hired at PepsiCo where she has worked for ten years in a variety of marketing roles. She expressed gratitude to PepsiCo for facilitating her time away when Scott was ill and after the birth of their two children. "Part of the way I deal with things—like having children and Scott's health challenges—is to compartmentalize," she said. She explained further:

So, I see work as separate from my personal life. I don't hide anything from my colleagues or my boss. When Scott had the transplant, I took a week off. The folks at work gave me flexibility to have more but working—at least a part of the day—actually helped me. It kept my mind occupied and focused on something else that was certainly less important, but it helped me get through every day. They were very understanding.

The turning point in Scott's health came right after he and Stacy married. He needed to be hospitalized more often, which Stacy said was very scary:

It was a roller coaster of emotions. He'd go into the hospital, get treatment, get much better, and come home. For a period of time, he'd be fine and then he'd get worse again. Over time, he didn't recover to the same level as before. The treatments were getting less effective and he was hospitalized more often. We knew there would be a time we'd need to talk about a transplant. It was clear he wasn't getting better. At that point he got on the transplant list. We met Dr. Arcasoy and the rest of the team at Columbia Presbyterian [Hospital]. We went through the orientation and spoke to a lot of people. It was scary and encouraging because we knew there was a way for him to come out healthy again. While he was on the list, he continued to deteriorate. He needed oxygen. We had oxygen in the house. I felt frightened. Especially during the eight months we were waiting for the transplant. In the back of my mind, I was worried what would happen if he didn't get one. I was very frightened. Every time the phone rang, every morning, I'd say, "Maybe this is the day." It never occurred to me that it wasn't going to work. I just knew it would. Scott and I didn't talk about it. We knew what each other was thinking and feeling and we tried to make every day as normal as possible.

Scott's transplant coordinator called him in three times for potential transplants. Each time, he and Stacy immediately went to the hospital. For a variety of reasons, problems with the offered lungs caused Scott's doctors to reject the organs. "Every time we went to the hospital and didn't get one, it was crushing for both of us," Stacy said. "We knew it was possible that this would take a while and the team at the hospital helped us manage our expectations. We just tried to stay positive."

Stacy and Scott experienced the ups and downs of the entire transplant process together, as one unit:

I knew I wasn't having a lung transplant but I certainly felt the emotional impact. The three times we went in thinking we were going to get the transplant and then told it wouldn't work—that was the worst. It was crushing. You get your hopes up so much. I remember the drive to the hospital each of those three times—us being so optimistic. At the same time, you're preparing yourself for this surgery that is a very serious thing where anything can happen. So, all the emotions go with that and you prepare yourself. And then you find out that you need to go home and continue waiting. It was very, very difficult. It was crushing. It felt like a train on my chest. It was like a huge weight was about to be lifted off but instead the weight came crushing back down on me, on us. You felt like you just got kicked in the gut. Kicked really hard! My hopes were so high. Our hopes were so high. It felt crushing. When it was the fourth time, there was no way I actually thought it was going to happen. . . until they wheeled him in and told us it was for sure. Then I believed it.

When he was actually in surgery for the transplant—I don't remember if it was twelve or fifteen hours—I felt nervous but more I felt relief. I knew that if he didn't have the surgery, it wouldn't end well so the upside of the surgery was so up. I felt really optimistic and hopeful. I didn't sleep a wink or eat a bite during those twelve to fifteen hours but never for a minute did I think we'd get bad news.

When I first saw him in the recovery room, it was jarring. He was still unconscious. He was hooked up to a lot of machines. It was great to see him breathing. The next time I saw him, I could see the change. It was the day after the transplant. I asked him, "How do you feel?" and he said, "Great!" It was amazing! He hadn't felt great in five years. To hear him say that meant so much. It felt to him like he was taking a real breath for the first time, a full breath. It was one of the most wonderful moments and from that point on I knew it was going to be okay. I had prepared myself that even if he felt better he might not look better. But he looked so much better so quickly. Right away, he looked good. He had color in his face. He had a different energy about him that it was really positive and healthy. I hadn't expected for it to be that instantaneous. It felt like a miracle. Absolutely. When

you see it live, the transformation is just incredible. To get back
to the person I knew when we first met, it felt like a miracle.

Scott's transplant took place in July of 2010. Six months later, he and Stacy started talking about having children. "We were getting older," Stacy said. "Scott was doing great. We wanted to bring children into this world. We thought we'd be pretty great parents and we felt we'd make great kids. We wanted to live a full life. Whatever happened in the future, we knew that there would be a lot of love in those children's lives."

Stacy and Scott's bond is so close, their relationship is one where "I" and "you" transform into "we." This included pregnancy. Since Scott's transplant, they have had two children. "When I was pregnant, I felt that *we* were pregnant. I don't think Scott gained weight," she said laughing, "but he felt he gave birth to our children as much as I did."

"When I had my kids, I had four months of maternity leave and then went back to working full time. Working is really important to me. It's important that I continue to advance in my career and that I'm a strong role model for my daughter and son," she said.

Stacy met John and Jilayne Bovill when she and Scott visited the Bovills at their home in New Jersey. "When we met John and Jilayne—the positive energy from them—it just lifted both of our spirits. It made Scott even healthier. Knowing them made his recovery faster. The incredible, wonderful people who they are, who Michael obviously was, having a part of him, made us feel better."

Before Stacy and Scott's first child, Brooke, was born, they asked John and Jilayne permission to name her after Michael. "There's a practice in Judaism that you give a Hebrew name to your child after a relative who has passed away," Stacy said as she cried. "We gave our daughter the Hebrew name Michaela after Michael. You do that for a relative. We very much feel that Michael is a part of our family. The naming ceremony was very special. John and

Jilayne and two of their daughters and all of our other family were there. This a small way to acknowledge an incredible gift."

As a transplant recipient, Scott will continue to see his pulmonologist, Dr. Selim Arcasoy, for the rest of his life. Given Scott and Stacy's committed relationship, Stacy will have a lifelong relationship to Dr. Arcasoy as well. "It's a special relationship we have with him," she said. "He has a really nice balance of being honest and transparent, not sugarcoating and having an optimistic spirit and being extremely comforting. Knowing Scott is in his care, we feel lucky."

Scott hoped that one outcome of receiving his transplants was that his self-acknowledged poor-quality singing would improve. When asked about his singing now, Stacy laughed:

> Scott is still a terrible singer but is happy to sing. When he gets his bronchoscopies [where he receives anesthesia], he doesn't quite know what's going on. Dr. Arcasoy told us that Scott was still under anesthesia and singing loudly, entertaining all the doctors. Dr. Arcasoy got a kick out of it. Scott sings in the car, around the house, with the kids. My daughter is also a terrible singer. She and Scott love to sing together. Sometimes, the three of us sing and dance together and our one-year-old son—who doesn't know many words—says "No, no, no!" We have a good time. We'll perform for each other. Just not on the big stage.

After overcoming this serious obstacle, Stacy and Scott are content with where their lives are now. "We're very grateful for where we are. Who knows what the future holds? It doesn't matter because we're happy today."

Whatever the future holds, one thing is clear: Stacy is signed up to be an organ donor.

SCOTT TAFFET'S PULMONOLOGIST

This story can be told in one sentence: The lungs of a devout Christian who died in a motorcycle accident are implanted into the chest of a self-acknowledged Jew facilitated by a Muslim transplant pulmonologist. Here's the longer story...

Dr. Selim Arcasoy, the transplant pulmonologist from the short story above knows a tremendous amount about his patients. Almost all that information is critical for his work as a physician. There is one thing that he doesn't know and one thing that he does not need to know. He claims they make no difference to him. "I don't look at their insurance. And I don't need to know their religion."

Dr. Arcasoy's roots in the practice of medicine are deep. "My father was a physician, a pediatric cardiologist. So, I grew up with him working and realized that's what I wanted to do," he said. "Dad was a good role model for a bedside physician. When my brother [now a practicing hematologist/oncologist] and I were children, occasionally, we'd go with him to his office."

Both of Dr. Arcasoy's parents were born in Turkey. His father was completing his training at the University of Seattle where Dr. Arcasoy and his brother were born. When Dr. Arcasoy was two years old, his father accepted a professorship at Hacettepe University Medical School in Ankara, Turkey. "So, I grew up in Turkey," he said. He and his brother both attended medical school at the same university where their father taught so that father and sons shared the morning car ride to school. "In Turkey, you start medical school at age eighteen and I finished in 1990 when I was twenty-four." He has now been a physician for more than half of his life. "I never considered that before," he said with a laugh.

Dr. Arcasoy's wife is a physician whose specialty was anesthesia and pain management. She now runs her own medical aesthetics practice. "She makes people look better," he said. He and his wife are parents of a son and daughter. With the legacy of a grandfather, uncle, mother, and father who are all physicians, Dr. Arcasoy reflected on the likelihood of his children following this career path:

> I don't know what the predictors are for children of physicians becoming physicians because my children want nothing to do with practicing medicine. My son is interested in engineering. My daughter is younger, but doesn't want to go into medicine. Maybe it skips generations. I'm generally a happy person. I come home after a long day at work and tell my family about something exciting that happened, some patient we helped or something sad that happened, someone passed away or got sick. They've heard all these stories. Maybe they heard too much [laughs]. I don't know.
>
> I trained in internal medicine at first. In that training, you experience different sub-specialties. In the second year of training, we select a sub-specialty—that's when we apply for a fellowship. The two fields I liked were hematology and pulmonary/critical

medicine. It was the critical care part that drew me into the field. You're learning to treat people who are really seriously ill in intensive care units. You have to have an expansive knowledge of medicine—whether it's respiratory failure or diabetic coma or gastro-intestinal bleeding or some neurologic catastrophe. You have to know about treatment of critically ill patients. As I was training in this field at the University of Pittsburgh, I got introduced to transplant medicine. On the very first day of my fellowship, I encountered a lung transplant patient. That drew me into practicing advanced lung disease and lung transplantation. What drew me in was that I found the lungs to be really interesting and vital organs and I could help patients who are helpless otherwise. These patients have pretty much exhausted all other treatment options and they come to us to see if they can get help to live longer, to have better quality of life. If we're able to achieve that, it's incredibly gratifying. Unfortunately, not all the stories have a happy ending. But the happy endings make us go forward and keep doing what we do. That's a big draw to this work.

Dr. Arcasoy refers to himself as a workaholic. That may be an understatement.

I have three main responsibilities. One is patient care—that is seeing patients and caring for them before and after transplant. This includes outpatients and office hours. I see patients with tough-to-diagnose issues. This also includes inpatient care and procedures. I may see post-patients from one day to twenty-plus years post-lung transplant. I also perform bronchoscopies which is a procedure that allows me to inspect the airways and lungs internally, take culture and biopsy samples to look for rejection and infection.

As medical director of the lung transplant program of Columbia University Medical Center, his second responsibility is administrative. "We are a team of forty to fifty people."

The third element of Dr. Arcasoy's staggering "job" is clinical research. He collaborates with colleagues investigating clinical research questions which come up as they care for patients.

In addition to what he refers to as his "main" responsibilities, he spoke about his father's influence on him as a practitioner:

The other thing I like to do is something which I may have learned from my father. Two days a week, I try to visit my patients who are hospitalized to say hi and answer their questions. I know what's happening to them because I follow them remotely, but I do what I call "social visits." The patients appreciate it. I fit these visits in between procedures. Somehow my schedule works out.

I've learned to do things efficiently. I start early. I'm at my office by six thirty in the morning and I leave when I'm done, that's not before six thirty in the evening. Having a wife and two kids adds to the challenge. I cycle a lot. I incorporated that into my life a couple of years ago. I commute to work on a bicycle when it's warm, two or three times a week. It's twenty miles each way. I get more tired but I feel a lot better when I do that. Lately, on my procedure days, I try to get out a little early and just exercise. It makes me feel better. I used to work a lot at night, but I've slowed down on that. I try to watch television or read the newspaper and be with my family. I get to my emails late at night because I have no time during the day. Spending time with my family helps balance things. I like what I do so that makes it easier. I really do like my job.

What does bother me is a lack of sleep but it's something I'm used to. Sometimes, the calls to consider a donor come in at two in the morning. Today is a tired day for me. I was in an all-day meeting reviewing new technology related to lung transplantations in Boston. I traveled the night before after my office hours. And then I flew back to New York. Then I went from the airport to an event I was scheduled to attend. It took longer to get to the event because of traffic than it did flying from Boston. I made it home at ten in the evening. It was a long day. I don't know what the state of my adrenal glands [glands that regulate stress] is. I think they're functioning.

I've had some issues with my knees. I had knee surgery in 2010. It didn't go well. After surgery, I had bleeding in my knee three times. It's like Murphy's Law. As a physician you have minor surgery and you get complications. That put me down a lot. My leg turned weaker and thinner. I turned forty-five the following year. That's when my wife bought me a bicycle and that really turned my life around a lot. I got in shape. I really loved it. I've met a lot of people who have nothing to do with medicine and we cycle together. I was able to do a couple of stages of the Tour de France. They are the mountainous stages of the Tour that amateurs like me do. One was in the French Alps. One was in the Pyrenees. They're like one hundred-mile rides but you're climbing 15,000 feet all in one day. Achievements like that, feeling fit enough to do that make me feel good.

It's helpful that Dr. Arcasoy is fit enough to ride in the Tour de France because the process of a lung transplant requires stamina of the transplant recipient and transplant pulmonologist. "The first step is for a patient to get listed," explained Dr. Arcasoy. He continued:

It involves evaluation with a lung doctor and a transplant coordinator. If the patient seems to be a reasonable candidate based on that evaluation, they undergo testing and consultations. This includes a detailed psycho-social evaluation, being seen by the surgeon, having their insurance and medication coverage

reviewed. Typically, it's a four- or five-day process. As a team
we review the findings. We do this weekly. Takes about two
hours to get through all our patients. We review their clinical
characteristics as well as their mental and physical wellbeing,
compliance, commitment, their medical and psycho-social
eligibility. "Social" means social support of family and friends
who will support them and be close by. It's very hard for a single
person to be a transplant patient on his or her own. We decide if
they need to be listed right then and there or if they could wait.
The current lung allocation system is score-based. Patients are
listed based on how sick they are. They receive scores ranging
from zero to one hundred. Sicker patients get higher values.
Average waiting time in this region is six to seven months.
At some point, you may be ranked number three but if there are
new sicker people, you may get pushed down the list or vice versa.

When a potential donor is identified, Dr. Arcasoy and his
teammates electronically review the donor information. Depending
on the remote evaluation, they decide whether to travel to physically
examine the organ. The surgeon, pulmonologist, and transplant
coordinator all participate in this decision-making process. When
all reviews of the lung or lungs are positive, if the recipient is not
already an inpatient, they are called and instructed to go to the
hospital. The patient is prepped for surgery. The physician gives the
patient information about the risks and benefits of the transplant
(informed consent). Patients retain the right to make decisions
about their own health and medical conditions. Assuming all
systems are a go, the procurement team drives or flies to where the
donor hospital is to inspect the lung or lungs which are still in the
chest of the donor.

Most donors are brain dead. By US law, when a patient is
declared brain dead, he or she is considered legally dead. "Brain
dead means you have no meaningful brain function compatible

with life," said Dr. Arcasoy. He explained the difficult decisions and next steps a family must take when a loved one becomes brain dead:

You cannot live like that. If you are taken off the respirator, you stop breathing. In the case of a donor who has severe neurologic injury with no chance of meaningful recovery (massive stroke or massive brain injury) they may not be brain dead but still legally qualify to be an organ donor. Donors are removed from the ventilator. If the heart stops within a pre-specified time period, then organs are harvested for transplantation. All of this requires approval of the donor's family. If the donor is going to donate multiple organs, you have to coordinate multiple teams for different organs. There may be heart, liver, kidney, pancreas, small intestine teams. There may be one lung team—if the lungs will be donated to one patient [as in the case of Scott Taffet], or two teams—if the lungs will be donated to two recipients. The same is true for kidneys. All of these teams are coordinated to go to the operating room at the same time to procure their respective organs. There is order to it, but it all occurs at the same time. It is a pretty intense process.

Our patient [the recipient] is waiting at our hospital. Our procurement team is out there assessing the donor lungs. They review the history, physiologic, and radiologic data. When the donor surgery starts, they inspect the donor lungs externally and internally. They make sure there is no pneumonia or contusions, that all the lobes expand nicely, that the oxygen levels are preserved, that internally the airways are clear, that they're not inflamed. They report all these findings to our surgeon with the recipient. We decide if the lung is satisfactory to be transplanted. If it's satisfactory, the procurement team procures the lung or lungs. They follow a special procedure to preserve the lungs which is to fill the lungs with a specially formulated preservative solution and put them on ice in a sterile bag. In a coordinated fashion, the team with the recipient starts the operation. We want to make sure that the recipient is as ready as possible when the lungs arrive so that the lungs can be implanted [stitched in] as soon as possible into the recipient to limit the time they're outside the body. The longer the lungs are outside the body, particularly extending beyond six to eight hours, the higher the chance of injury to the lungs and malfunction or lack of function after the transplant. The timing of the initiation of the recipient surgery depends on the travel time for the donor team. There have been times we have flown to Puerto Rico to get lungs. That's a five-hour flight so the surgery for the recipient doesn't start right away. Generally, it takes one to two hours of surgery to get the recipient ready for their lungs to be removed. The surgical team opens the chest. If needed, they relieve the lungs of any kind of adhesions to prepare them for explantation [surgical removal]. The recipient is stabilized while the donor lungs are in transit. The implant surgery takes four to five hours for a single-lung transplant and about six to eight hours for a double-lung transplant. Then the patient is taken to the intensive care unit.

The transplant surgical team is a critical element of the transplant process that is essentially contained within a twenty-four-hour period. Typically, Dr. Arcasoy does not participate in the actual surgery. During this period, his role is to help decide on which recipients will be the best fit for an available lung or lungs, whether the donor lungs are satisfactory, and helping the surgeon make last-minute decisions if there are questions about organ quality.

In his twenty-plus years as a pulmonologist, Dr. Arcasoy has seen, examined, and worked with many lungs—both inside and outside the bodies of his patients. "It's really remarkable to see," he said. "When you have a patient on full support, trying to keep the person alive—it's not easy while under general anesthesia when the lungs are so bad—and you put new lungs in and, all of a sudden, in most cases the physiology gets better and that's really remarkable." Dr. Arcasoy has many years of experience working with lungs, and continues to be fascinated by them:

> What I do most procedurally is bronchoscopies on living patients—like Scott—so I see the inside of the airways and lungs. I've been doing this since 1994 so it's become kind of routine. When I was in training, I used ex-planted lungs—lungs that were diseased and removed from patients—for research. Seeing the lungs outside the body is really remarkable. It's shocking for someone who has never seen that. It's really cool. That's something my kids would say.

Dr. Arcasoy navigates the sensitive balance of needing to be clinically exact while working with human beings who happen to be profoundly sick:

> The foundation of what we do is recognize the patient is a person. At least, that's what I do. That patient comes first. Whatever we do, we consider the best interests of that patient. Sometimes this is tough. We can't predict everything and we make these high-stakes decisions because we're very worried that this patient is at very high risk of dying. So, we might have an offer for that patient with lungs that have some issues. They're not perfect. Maybe the oxygen exchange is impaired. Maybe there's a small focus of infection or trauma. Maybe there's some other medical problem. Maybe the donor used IV drugs in the past or is using them currently. We would be devastated if there is donor-transmission of infection. How do you make that decision? How do you balance the risk of that happening versus the risk of your

candidate dying on the waiting list? These are not light decisions. I really struggle with this sometimes. If the risk is not warranted, I'd rather not take it. If the risk is warranted, it would be done with the full consent of the patient. I might say to a patient, "Hey, we have great lungs but they're from a drug user and there's less than a one in one hundred chance that a bad infection may be transmitted." Then it's up to the patient how to proceed. Years ago, we transplanted a cystic fibrosis patient—who is still around—with a lung from a donor with malignant brain cancer but our patient was about to die. So, with that circumstance, it made sense to take the risk and we were fortunate. I don't always know what the right answers are, but we try to find them in each case to the extent possible.

Our exposure to the donor history is very mechanical and becomes routine. We're looking at all the technical stuff. Having said that, recently I've experienced cases of young people—a couple from my own community—who died from drug overdose. A couple of them, my kids knew from their school district. That's an eye opener on many levels. It reminds you that these were unfortunate people who had a devastating injury. You also feel that this is your kid's acquaintance or friend. So it shows you how fragile life is. I preach to our patients about the gift they get from donors. I use that as a reason why they should do their best to take care of themselves. "This is a precious gift and someone died in order for you to get it so you make sure that you take care of it." In my day-to-day life, unfortunately, I do not think about each and every donor. Usually, it's a middle of the night call from my surgical colleague. "This is what happened to the person. He or she is this age. Here is the technical data. What do you think we should do?" Because of the nature of our business, the timing of the calls, the urgency with which we need to make a decision, we don't spend too much time on who the donor was as a person.

"Some people accept organs if they need them but don't sign up to be donors. I believe the best people to promote organ donations are the organ recipients and their families." He paused and added, "I signed up to be an organ donor. So has my family."

While facing the reality of the demands of his work, Dr. Arcasoy succeeds in knowing his patients as individuals. "I've known Scott [Taffet] for a long time," he said. "He's a super guy. Low key. Unassuming. Really nice person. When you get to know him, he jokes around, has a very witty personality. And he's a quiet person. Except when he has been given sedative medications before a bronchoscopy, he may even sing then. He doesn't talk that much but when he does, he says important stuff. He's private."

His encounters with Scott extend well beyond the examining table:

I like to do these long bike rides. One time, on a Saturday, I rode to Montauk with a friend of mine whose name—coincidentally—is Scott. We stop to eat and drink and I see my patient, Scott, walking towards us with his wife and baby. I'm in my biking gear, lycra, helmet, glasses. But we both recognize each other and have a good laugh. Scott is involved with the Lung Transplant Project, a foundation our patients started to help raise funds for research to help improve the lives of transplant patients. I've seen him outside of the medical office where we discuss how to do the work of the foundation. We have conversations about him going back to his life, working as a lawyer, having his children—which is great for me to see. Here was someone who was going to die years ago and now is productive with a family. It's wonderful.

Dr. Arcasoy identifies himself as a Muslim. He now knows that Scott identifies himself as a Jew. He recently learned that the donor of the lungs now expanding and contracting in Scott's chest came from someone who identified himself as Christian. To Dr. Arcasoy, it is simple: "Religion should not matter how we treat each other in medicine or outside of medicine," he said. "We're all human."

RECIPIENT OF ONE OF MICHAEL'S KIDNEYS, AND SOCORRO MORAN, DIANA'S MOTHER

"**M**iracle" is a big word that deserves extraordinary circumstances to be properly used. Diana Flores-Moran has experienced a series of life-threatening health conditions throughout her young life. I believe that "miracle" is an accurate description given that she is alive and relatively well.

Diana's Mexican-born mother, Socorro Moran, was six-and-a-half months pregnant at Diana's birth in Staten Island, New York on January 10, 2003. Diana weighed two pounds, six ounces. "She grew and was doing well. Everything looked okay," Socorro said in her native Spanish. As it became evident later, the initial appearance of wellness was an illusion and Diana's survival is a testament to her mother's iron will, courage, and a host of answered prayers.

Despite regularly seeing pediatricians, Socorro reported that the doctors never told her Diana had any problems. As far as Socorro knew and could see, Diana was overcoming her early birth. "Everything was normal. She gained weight. She grew up." The appearance of wellness changed when Diana turned six. "She developed asthma but it seemed under control," Socorro said. Then Diana began to cough persistently:

The cough was strong and it was every day. I had to take her several times to the emergency room. We went to two different hospitals. They [emergency room doctors] gave my daughter nebulizers and antibiotics. They never told me that something else was going on. I don't know if they were keeping the information from me or were just neglectful in examining Diana. They only spoke about the cough and asthma and that's all they treated. Then Diana was in a crisis for one month. I had to spend every night with her on my lap. It was the only way she could sleep.

On November 30th, 2009, I took my daughter to the pediatrician. She was so sick that I asked the doctor to admit her to the hospital [Saint Vincent Hospital in Staten Island]. I told the doctor they needed to do more tests, look more, because Diana was so sick. The doctor said "No, let's wait and see what happens in two days." I didn't accept it. I fought with the doctor. I said strong words to her. Security people from the hospital came. I kept telling them they had to admit my daughter to the hospital. When all this happened, my life changed. I thought, My daughter needs me now and I have to stand for her. I am very Catholic. I asked the Virgin Guadalupe [Mary, mother of Jesus] to give me strength to face this situation. Guadalupe responded to my prayer. Guadalupe was with me and my family. Finally, they admitted Diana. Several doctors examined her.

As Socorro spoke, I found myself in awe of this woman whose mothering instinct superseded any hesitation she might have experienced facing doctors and security staff who possessed power and authority over her and her daughter's fate. Socorro, an immigrant to the United States from Mexico, whose English is weak, would simply not accept what she considered to be inadequate care for her sick child. For the first time in my life, I was grateful to Mary, who inspired Socorro's heroic actions.

The next day, Diana stopped breathing for ten to fifteen seconds. Socorro was with Diana when it happened:

Diana had a big, deep, strong exhalation and then she didn't breathe in. The nurse said, "She stopped breathing!" I cried out, "No! Diana, no!" They were about to do something to make her breathe but Diana came back. The doctors told me to leave the room and I didn't want to. I told them, "I will stay here! I will not leave my daughter!" And I stayed. The doctors put an oxygen mask on Diana and checked her heart. That's when they told me that Diana's heart is very delicate and they don't have the equipment to properly treat her here. They said she needs to go to another better equipped hospital. An ambulance took Diana and me to Columbia Presbyterian in Manhattan. Diana was connected to so many things. I kept thinking, This is taking too long! I am going to lose my daughter! When we arrived at Columbia Presbyterian, there were a lot of doctors waiting. They told me that Diana had many serious problems and that they didn't have much hope that she would overcome this. When they told me this, I asked Guadalupe to help my daughter, to stop her suffering. I said to the Virgin, "I will give you my daughter if you stop her suffering and her pain. If that will stop the pain, I will accept that."

The doctor told me that Diana's heart was very delicate and fragile. They felt that they could not biopsy her kidneys because she might not be able to come back after the anesthesia. They also said they could not perform dialysis because of this weakness of her heart. I was confused why they were talking about dialysis and kidneys. I didn't know anything about kidney problems before. They waited a day and did the biopsy and confirmed that Diana's kidneys were not working.

From December 1, 2009 until July 17, 2010 (the day Diana received a kidney transplant), Socorro spent most of her time with Diana at Columbia Presbyterian. Every day, Socorro traveled from her home in Staten Island to Manhattan to be with Diana. According to Socorro, Diana never received dialysis but did receive "a lot of medications."

Diana only remembers the coughing, but little else of this period. She said, "It was hard being in the hospital all that time. I didn't see my friends. I did have my mom. My brothers visited me on weekends."

Diana's biological father left the family when Socorro was pregnant with Diana and never returned. (In addition to Diana, Socorro is mother to two sons and one other daughter. Diana is the youngest.) When Diana was one, Socorro met Elidio Flores, who helped raise Diana. Socorro and Elidio later married. "He [Elidio] has been the father for Diana," Socorro said. "Diana knew him as her father. But as she was growing up, something was not right for her. We told her the whole story after the transplant when she was eleven. She recognizes him as her father. He supported us through all our struggles."

Even though I did not meet or speak with Elidio, I felt huge respect for him. Elidio stood by Socorro and Diana through years of Diana's illness and Socorro's attention/devotion to her child. I admired his strength, perseverance, and commitment.

During Diana's hospitalization, Socorro took tests to see if she could donate a kidney to her daughter. "It wasn't possible because

I wasn't taking good care of myself during this time," Socorro said. Being there for her daughter while she was hospitalized, along with the stress of the situation, took a toll on Socorro's health:

> Every day I commuted from Staten Island to Manhattan. I had to take buses, subways, and a ferry. It took one and a half hours each way. I got anemia. Because of the anemia, I was too weak to be a donor. The doctors said, "You have to overcome the anemia and then we'll see." It was a Friday in July [July 16th, 2010] and the doctor told us, "We have a compatible kidney. Do you want her to have this kidney or do you want to wait until you get better and you can be the donor?" I decided it would be better to take this kidney now because my daughter was suffering for too long. I wanted to see her well. The doctors told me that Diana's heart was weak and even if the kidney transplant went well, her heart was so weak that she might need a heart transplant, too. They explained the risk of Diana possibly rejecting the kidney. There were many, many things to face. I asked Guadalupe, the Virgin, for my daughter. I asked for her to get better. I told Guadalupe, "If Diana gets better, I will be grateful. But if she's not going to get better, please take her with you now. I will accept your will. You decide. I just want Diana's suffering to end."

Socorro decided to accept the donated kidney. On Saturday, July 17th, the transplant operation began at five in the morning. At two in the afternoon, the surgeon told Socorro that the surgery was complete and that Diana was stable.

> I went to see her. When I saw her, I cried a lot. Diana was connected to many things—tubes, machines everywhere. When Diana woke up, she asked me for water. She was so thirsty. The doctor told me that I could not give her water. We could take an ice cube and touch her lips with it. Diana's brother did that.

My family asked me to go home to rest and I went home. Her brothers stayed with Diana. That evening, they called me and said, "They took out all the tubes from Diana's body and Diana just ate rice with shrimp."

I felt happy and relieved to know that Diana had her first meal. And then I started praying that Diana's body would not reject the kidney and that everything go well for her. It went well. Every year since then, every July 17ᵗʰ, we celebrate Diana's "kidney birthday." That's the day Diana was born again.

It was during our interview when Diana, at the age of fourteen, and Socorro learned the name of the donor of her kidney, Michael Bovill. It was also the first time Diana heard Socorro tell the story of her illnesses.

"I haven't heard any of this before," Diana said. "To hear it is kinda like interesting. I'm happy to know it. I was interested before, but we didn't talk about it. I am grateful to Michael that I have another life. I am grateful to his parents for their hard decision to donate his organs."

When she learned the identity of her donor, Diana asked me about Michael. I wondered if I was the right person to tell her about Michael. I never met him, but had become immersed in his biography. Diana was so sincere, so very interested. She struck me as innocent and genuinely loving-hearted. I had no idea if and when people who had known the living Michael would tell this young woman—whose continuing life was made possible by a kidney now efficiently filtering her blood that had previously filtered Michael's—about her donor.

I sensed that it was proper that I tell her what I knew about Michael. I told her stories his parents, sister, and fellow members of the Coast Guard told me—how he finished tied for last in training exercises in boot camp because he hung back to help his fellow recruits who were struggling; how he filled the gas tank of his mother's car on the day of his accident; how his admiral met him briefly yet was so impressed; how everyone who knew him remarked about his smile. I told Diana that she was one of the five recipients of Michael's organs. She asked the names of her fellow recipients and I told her stories about Roxanne and Scott. (At that point, I knew almost nothing about Elijah and Zhou.)

Diana expressed pleasure to know about Michael, particularly his smile and the kindness he regularly displayed to stranger and friend alike. "I feel thankful to receive one of his organs. I'm happy to know Michael's name." Despite not knowing his name before, Diana felt a deep connection to Michael:

I always had Michael and his family in my mind. Feeling grateful to them, praying for them. The decision for Michael to be a donor must have been difficult for them. They are always in my prayers. Until today, I did not know Michael's name, but I was always thinking of him. I would love to meet Michael's parents. I want to thank them in person. I sent many blessings to his family. I'd like a photo of Michael. I would place it between the images of my saints because he saved many lives. I have paintings and sculptures of nine saints on the wall of my bedroom.

Since her transplant, Diana's medical journey is eased but not simple. Fluid accumulated in her ears. This caused difficulty with her hearing. She had surgery to implant drainage tubes in her ears. Every year, the tubes are surgically replaced. Socorro reported that Diana now hears well. She wears braces which makes speaking clearly a bit difficult for her. She is still diagnosed with asthma. "She's fourteen years old, and she's not growing as she should," Socorro said. She is four feet, eleven inches tall and weighs 105 pounds. Diana does play basketball a little, but "I stop because I get tired quickly. I experience asthma. I have a special physical education class where I do push-ups against a wall. I don't ride a bicycle but I do jump rope."

"School is good for me," Diana, who is fluent in English and Spanish, said. She continued:

I go to I.S. 49 [Berta A. Dreyfus] in Staten Island. I have good grades. I'd like to become a nurse or a teacher. For fun, I hang out with my friends, but I don't go far from my house when it's dark. Sometimes we eat junk food. Sometimes we eat like healthy food because I don't want high blood pressure. My favorite musician is Alex Aiono. He's a YouTuber (someone who makes videos seen on YouTube). I like Italian food because my dad is a chef and sometimes he makes food for my birthday. For my last birthday, we had chicken marsala, chicken francaise, baked ziti, pasta with shrimp. For breakfast I drink coffee but not that much. Sometimes, my mom makes waffles. Sometimes, I eat Mexican bread. I don't watch TV that much. My favorite book is Diary of a Wimpy Kid. *It's about a boy who struggles to fit in when he's in middle school.*

Since the transplant, every year Socorro and Diana make a pilgrimage to the Basilica of Our Lady of Guadalupe in Mexico City. It is the most visited Catholic pilgrimage site in the world. "When Diana was so sick and I prayed to the Virgin, I promised her that if my daughter accepts the organ and it goes well, we will go to Mexico to visit the Virgin in her house, to thank the Virgin," Socorro said.

"When I go there, I am thankful," Diana said. "I ask the priest to give me blessing. I take holy water at the church and I leave flowers. I bring gifts for friends and family in the United States and the priest blesses them with holy water. The gifts are key chains and necklaces with saints and the Virgin on them."

Since her transplant, Diana experiences visions. "When one of my uncles got sick, he went to the hospital," Socorro said. She continued to explain:

Diana and I went to visit him. When I thought it was time to leave, Diana said, "No, we have to stay." I told her, "We have to go. Too much time in the hospital is not good for you." So we left and Diana was crying. She said to me, "He's going to die. We need to stay with him." When we got home, I got a call from my cousin at the hospital saying that my uncle had just passed away.

Another time, the mother of one my neighbors got sick. Diana and I went to visit the woman at the hospital. When I thought it was time to leave, Diana said, "Let's stay longer." I told her, "Too much time in the hospital is not good for you." When we got home, Diana took a shower. After the shower, she came to me and said, "The mother of our neighbor just passed away. I just saw that." A few minutes later, I got a call from my friend saying her mother had just passed away.

Diana regularly sees and speaks with what Socorro calls "a being." Socorro described the being:

It's a good one. They have conversations. Diana and I sleep in the same room that's divided by a curtain. I hear her talking with the being. We call him "Seraphim." During the day, Diana sees him but they don't talk. She'll tell me that she just saw him over there or he's doing this or that. I tell her, "Okay, that's fine. He's just playing." During the night, when she's sleeping, she speaks with him and I can hear when they talk. Sometimes Diana speaks English, sometimes Spanish. It's hard to understand because she's sleeping. I know she's talking with Seraphim because sometimes, she says his name so I know she's not just dreaming. Because of this being, I feel it is good that Diana knows more about Michael and his family. This being is a young man, fourteen or fifteen years old.

Diana added, "His hair is a light coffee color. He's tall and thin. I can't say what color his skin is. I can't see him well. He's like a shadow."

Reflecting on Diana's early years, Socorro is disappointed in how things transpired.

> I think the care my daughter received before the transplant was poor. They were negligent. They didn't tell me that whole situation. They didn't give me all the information. Had Diana received better care, I think it would have prevented the situation that happened. I think that if we were in a better financial situation, the care would have been better. They would have paid more attention to me and my daughter. They didn't care too much. I don't think that if we had been white, the care would have been better. The poor care had to do with our economic situation.

"I tell Diana that God sends his best soldiers to war," said Socorro, "and you are one of God's best soldiers."

The same could be said about Socorro.

DR. NAMRATA JAIN

DIANA'S PEDIATRIC NEPHROLOGIST

D r. Namrata Jain had the innocent idea that her first Mother's Day as the mother of her almost one-year-old son would be relatively quiet. She planned to spend it with her son and husband. That fantasy Mother's Day turned out quite differently.

Pediatric nephrologist (kidney specialist) Dr. Jain was on-call that day. "I received two calls," she recalled. That was the start of a not-so-quiet Mother's Day:

The first was from the ICU to come in for an emergency dialysis. A young man had overdosed on lithium and needed immediate dialysis to get the toxins out. We performed the dialysis and he did well. Then I got another call from a transplant coordinator that one of my patients was getting a long-awaited transplant match the same day. That Mother's Day, I got to meet two moms. One was a mom who was grateful that her son survived a drug overdose and the other was a mom who was so grateful to have her child get a kidney transplant. So, it was a special Mother's

Day. For me, it ended up being the best Mother's Day—that I could help two other mothers. It was a good fantasy Mother's Day for the other moms.

Dr. Jain was born in India and came to the United States when she was four.

My parents came to study in the US for their PhDs. My dad came when I was six months old and my mom came when I was one. I lived with my grandparents and uncles and aunts in India until I came to the US My parents were still taking night classes when I arrived. My son doesn't have that experience because both my husband (also an MD) and I finished our training before he was born. I always want to make sure that my son knows that the nanny is not his mom. Hopefully, I'm doing a good job.

Both her mother and father's families are dominated by engineers. Dr. Jain came to a career in medicine informed by her family's career of choice.

I was an engineering undergrad with a minor in chemistry at the University of Pennsylvania. At Penn, my focus was bio-medical engineering. There was a pretty cool class where we worked with patients in hospitals. We'd go on patient rounds and observe in the operating room with cardio-thoracic surgeons. I really liked designing things and working with patients. I liked it so much, I started taking pre-med classes and applied to medical school in my senior year. It was kind of a windy path, but I found I really liked the patient care aspect. I was drawn to pediatrics because I had been working with kids since I was in high school. During summers, I was a camp counselor. I really loved working with children. It's an honor to take care of anyone's family member but it's a very special honor when a mom entrusts you with her child. When a parent gives me their child to care for, that child becomes my child. You try not to become too personal. . . but it becomes very personal. I think of them as my kid, too. It helps me form a really great bond with the parents. They know I'll do everything for their kid as I'd do for my own.

The family connection to engineering led Dr. Jain to her specialty of kidney care.

In pediatrics, you rotate through different specialties. My mentor said to me, "You're an engineer. I think you'd like the kidneys. There's a lot of logic and math." I'm interested in flow and the vessels leading from the aorta to the kidney. Fluid mechanics come into play. I was intrigued. I really, really loved it. I really liked kidney transplants. It was very tangible. You've got two kidneys and you can donate one—which always seems amazing. It is such an amazing gift that people can share.

"I tell people to drink a lot of water, but I have not been as good a patient as I tell other people to be," she admitted, laughing. She advises transplant patients or a child with kidney stones to drink two to three liters of water a day (about sixty to ninety ounces). She reported that the day before she drank "about twenty-seven ounces. Definitely not the amount I should drink. I think what happens to most people in medicine is that we're running around and we'll bring our water bottle and then we leave it somewhere [laughs] and then you end up having to get another one."

Her background in engineering comes into play, too, with her children transplant patients. "Most of the time it's the kidney of an adult going into a child; it's a real estate issue because it's a larger kidney going into a smaller person," she said.

As a pediatric nephrologist at Columbia Presbyterian Hospital, one of Dr. Jain's responsibilities is to provide critical care for children in the ICU who have an injury or disease of the kidney—

some needing emergency dialysis, others requiring another form of treatment. "One of the aspects about being a pediatric nephrologist is that there are some mothers you meet for pre-natal consultation," she said. "If something shows up on a fetal ultrasound that gets our attention, you show up in their lives before birth. As they grow up, they may or may not need a transplant."

Her other responsibilities include teaching problem-based learning renal pathology for the medical students at Columbia Presbyterian Hospital; serving as the elective director for pediatric nephrology where she assists medical students who want certain training that might not be in their standard curriculum; and treating patients at Columbia Presbyterian's outpatient clinic. In addition to all her other tasks, Dr. Jain's commitment to her patients includes calling them with their lab results.

"The state of my adrenals (the glands responsible for dealing with stress) is probably hyper-mode," she said, punctuated with a long laugh. "I haven't tested my cortisol (a hormone that influences, regulates, or modulates the body's response to stress), but it's probably high." She laughed again. "It's part of my life."

Balancing her career as a doctor with parenting her son is a delicate tightrope dance for Dr. Jain:

> I had friends whose parents were doctors and they said, "I didn't get to hang out with my parents that much." I've been lucky to have awesome colleagues at Columbia. There's a really great team of nurses and nurse practitioners. But keep in mind, everything in medicine today is electronic medical records. I don't like typing notes in front of my patients. It's my particular style—probably makes me slower. So, I record my notes at home after my son is asleep. He has never seen me work on the computer.

In addition to working with donated organs, Dr. Jain is intimately acquainted with being a family member of an organ donor.

My aunt in Kansas City died suddenly and our family members made the decision to donate her organs. My cousins have received letters from recipients. It becomes more personal when you are on the other side [the donor family]. I think about my family deciding to donate my aunt's organs when I think about the donors whose organs we transplant. I think about what their families are going through and who they can save with their gift. It gives me the happy jitters recognizing the connection we have as humans no matter what we look like. It's this innate nature of wanting to help that crosses human boundaries.

I feel the presence of beauty, magic, and awe. I don't think for me that this work can ever be routine. Even when I get a phone call for a potential kidney, I feel a rush for everybody who has a second chance of life. I think of the donor family and what they've been through. I'm still awestruck every time.

Even though the primary doctor in the operating room is the surgeon, Dr. Jain frequently scrubs in to the actual transplant to check on the wellbeing of her patient and kidney that is in the process of becoming her patient's. "It's a real team effort," she said. She continued:

We know each other really closely. The surgeon knows I'm going to come in and make sure everything is okay. Sometimes, children need dialysis while they're in the process of getting their transplant! This is to make sure that all the electrolytes are safe until the new kidney begins to kick in. It's magical for me when the kidney starts to work and you start to see urine, you see their kidney numbers getting better. Some of these kids haven't eaten chocolate because of their prior lack of kidney function can lead to elevated potassium levels. So, when they are about to go home, I'll give them some candy or a chocolate cupcake. It's a treat for me.

Dr. Jain experiences a range of feelings when communicating with the parents of her patients. She describes variations of what she calls "a rush." "One kind of rush is when I call a parent and tell them that their child has the option of receiving a kidney *and* that's there's a match," she said. "It's one of the best phone calls ever. Each time it's a special rush. You see them coming in to get ready for the transplant—there are so many emotions. I feel my heart pounding."

"There's a different feeling to tell a parent that their child needs a transplant. You can see their whole world breaking down. It's not easy to be on dialysis. Kids often don't go to school regularly. Their grades get affected. It hinders their ability just to be a kid. And it turns the lives of their parents inside out," she said.

Dr. Jain has been Diana's pediatric nephrologist for three years. "She has been happily stable," Dr. Jain reported. She described Diana's progression and growth after having transplant surgery:

> *Some bumps in the road, but her kidney has been a rock for her. I see her once every one to two months. Over the years of working with Diana, I've seen her turning more into a pre-teen which is really fun. She was more quiet in the beginning. Now, she's applying nail polish and doing her hair. It's fun to see her have the chance to grow up and doing so. She is totally not self-absorbed. Our patients have gone through so much in their lives. They're so giving. I can definitely say that none of my patients are self-absorbed. It's quite remarkable how grounding their experiences have been. They're very much into their families.*

Typically, a child who is a kidney recipient will not go to school for the first two months after the transplant. During this time, Dr. Jain will see the child twice a week to monitor their drug levels. Then they come in once every two weeks, then once a month for the remainder of the first year. After that, they will see Dr. Jain once every two months with Dr. Jain reviewing their lab results once a month. If there's a medical concern—even a simple cold—they'll come in to be checked out. Usually, when a patient turns twenty-one, they transition to an adult specialist. Dr. Jain said the transition might be delayed if a patient needs a bit more hand holding, and she will continue to see them until they're ready to transition to the adult specialists. Kidney transplant recipients should receive follow-up for the rest of their lives.

The attention to detail and this lifelong care of her patients was instilled in Dr. Jain by one of her mentors, Dr. Bill Harmon.

He recited this quote: "The price of liberty is eternal vigilance." That is the amount of future-oriented meticulous attention that we try to use. To make sure our kids are safe. Sometimes, you might think things are fine and you find out they're not fine. That's why we make our patients come every month to get their lab work. If they have a rash or a cold or a cough, we know about it. It can become exhausting but regardless, I live by that quote.

After years of study and three years of intensive practice as a pediatric nephrologist, Dr. Jain is still fascinated by the kidney.

It's structure, function, and tissue—it's interesting to me. It's kind of like the brain in a way. You have about a million nephrons in each kidney. These are filtering units that you're born with, if born full term. Your kidney decides what to take out and leave in your blood. It decides on your metabolic balance and your pH, or acidity of your blood. It's the only place that produces a protein to tell your bone marrow to make red blood cells. Some people think it just makes urine, but it does a lot of other things too.

Clear communication is challenging in the best of circumstances. Given the life and death tensions that Dr. Jain addresses every day, having her patients and their parents understand what she is saying becomes even more challenging. Add to it that some of her patients and their families do not speak English, and her job becomes more challenging. In some cases, she and her team use an interpretor.

Regardless of the language, I can say that many times we say things and the parents just don't hear what you intended. In general—from the physician side—we try to repeat and document everything. I know when I've been a patient, I've heard something and interpret it as something else that the physician said or even what my husband (also a physician) heard. Sometimes, I communicate with a patient and think they got it and they didn't get it. So, you keep trying.

Diana's mother, Socorro, felt that Diana received inadequate care before coming to Columbia Presbyterian Hospital because of her family's financial situation. Socorro expressed only gratitude for the care Diana received at Columbia Presbyterian. Dr. Jain had not been at Columbia during Diana's initial evaluations and transplant.

Dr. Jain commented on the practices at her hospital:

We have many Medicaid patients. For us, it doesn't matter if you have insurance or don't. It speaks to the work of the finance and social work teams because they make it possible. We have transplanted undocumented patients. We try to see everybody for who they are. I think it's wonderful. It makes me able to do medicine that is good for our patients.

Dr. Jain spoke about her life and work the week before what would be her second Mother's Day as a mother. Given her first was spent performing an emergency dialysis and participating in a transplant, she laughed as she considered what she hoped for in the upcoming one. "My fantasy Mother's Day? This year I'm not on call. I'm just going to hang out with my son and husband," she said.

RECIPIENT OF MICHAEL'S LIVER

&

ELIJAH PARKER

RECIPIENT OF MICHAEL'S LEFT KIDNEY

Here's what is known about Zhou and Elijah:

- Zhou received Michael's liver.

- Elijah received Michael's left kidney.

- On the day of the transplants, July 17, 2010, Zhou was sixty-one or sixty-two years old and Elijah was eighteen.

- Both Zhou and Elijah attended an event hosted by LiveOnNY on June 1, 2011 where members of Michael's family met them and fellow organ recipients Roxanne Watson and Scott Taffet.

In an email dated May 10th, 2017, Maria Torres, manager of Donor Family Services at LiveOnNY wrote:

- Regarding Zhou: "Has not been seen since 2013. A no-show."
- Regarding Elijah: "Patient was on dialysis for two years and then left. They do not know this recipient's whereabouts."

Efforts to find contact information for Zhou and Elijah—initiated both in the United States and China—were unsuccessful. This included letters sent to two people named Elijah Parker found in a Google search of individuals with that name living in New York City and approximately the age the Elijah—the recipient of Michael's kidney—would be today.

John Bovill, Michael's father, and Scott Taffet, recipient of Michael's lungs, shared their recollections and impressions of Zhou and Elijah from their brief interactions at the event.

Sau Hwang, who translated for Zhou at the event, provided insight into Zhou which follows in the next chapter.

ZHOU YUAN LI

Both John Bovill and Scott Taffet reported that Zhou spoke no English, with the exception of the words "thank you."

"He was very grateful," Scott said. "He clasped his hands together in a gesture of thanks and said thank you many times to members of the Bovill family."

"He kept bowing to my mother," John said. "I think it was because she was the elder of our family. I saw a lot of compassion and thankfulness. I kept saying to the translator, 'He is so welcome.' What a gift. What an honor. He had tears in his eyes. He was very emotional."

Scott remembered Zhou crying. "I don't think we hugged. We're transplant recipients concerned about germs. Maybe we shook hands."

John reported hearing that Zhou returned to China. He did not remember the source of this information, but thought it might have been a member of the staff from LiveOnNY.

ELIJAH PARKER

Scott described Elijah as "a tall young man. Shy. Very kind eyes. Nice-looking kid. I don't remember a word he said. He and I didn't speak with each other. I remember Elijah seeing a photograph of Michael on his motorcycle and saying, 'That's really cool!' and Michael's aunt saying, 'No, it's really not that cool.'"

Jilayne Bovill, Michael's mother, and Mandy Lacy, Michael's sister, recalled when Elijah visited them at their respective homes in 2012 or 2013.

"He spent a night with us and then went down with Mandy to her home," Jilayne said.

"We went to Atlantic City, the beach, the boardwalk," Mandy said. "My cousin Joanna was with us. We did a bit of sightseeing. It's near where I live. He told me his mom is doing good. We enjoyed spending time together. He was a very sweet person. Very kind. Really polite. He told me that he was doing very well—that it was crazy that he never felt better in his life. Really energetic. With a little extra [laughs]. We had invited him to come to our place anytime. He was family. He had a part of Michael. Elijah was very grateful to Michael. I will always consider him part of our family."

After the visit, Mandy and Elijah communicated through Facebook for a few years. Mandy said that their last contact was about a year ago. "We were catching up. How he was doing. How we were doing. It was small talk. He said he was well. I don't think he had gone to college. The last time I heard, he wanted to go to culinary school. But I'm not sure if that happened or not," she said.

Elijah's mother attended the LiveOnNY gathering in 2011. She and John spoke there. "I remember her telling me that she prayed for a miracle," John said, "and the next day she got a phone call telling her that a kidney was available. [This was Michael's.] She had a deep faith and her prayers were answered by a phone call."

SAU HWANG
ZHOU'S TRANSLATOR

A s a fluent speaker of Cantonese, Mandarin, and English, as well as being a recipient of a liver transplant, Sau Hwang was uniquely qualified to translate for Zhou Yuan Li. Zhou, the recipient of Michael Bovill's liver, spoke only Cantonese, the dominant language of southeast China. He spoke almost no English and needed a translator for a gathering of three of his fellow organ recipients, Michael's parents, and family—none of whom spoke Cantonese. Sau, a volunteer at LiveOnNY, served as Zhou's translator on June 1st, 2011 when he, Roxanne Watson, Scott Taffet, and Elijah Parker met Michael's family at a donor family/organ recipients ceremony hosted by LiveOnNY in New York City. "I met him once," Sau recalled, "on the day of the ceremony. He was so skinny."

As a liver transplant recipient herself, Sau was in a remarkable position to understand Zhou's experience. "My transplant changed my life," she said. "Every day I can see the sun come up. I have seen my two kids graduate from college and seen them both get married and even see my grandchild. I feel happy and grateful to get a second life."

Sau was born in Shanghai and grew up speaking Mandarin, the dominant language throughout most of northern and southwestern

China. As a fourteen year old, she learned Cantonese when she moved to Hong Kong. In 1976, at the age of thirty, she moved to the United States where she learned English. In 1999, she received a liver transplant and began to volunteer for the New York Donors Network, which later became LiveOnNY.

Sau's desire to come to the United States began as a young girl. "It was my dream to come to the US," she said. "I had a classmate. Her father was in the US. She always got nice stuff from her father. So I thought that one day I need to come to the United States and become whatever I want to. I find that if you're a workaholic that will be true," she said laughing. "I learned English when I came to the United States. I'm still not very good. Most of the time, I learn by watching TV and reading newspapers. I didn't go to school. If I went to school, it would have been better."

Even though she didn't receive a formal education, Sau worked hard to build a life for herself. "When I came to the United States, I became a workaholic. Oh yes! Of course! I worked as a bookkeeper for a small company. I met a man from Taiwan and we got married. Once I had children, I stopped working until my younger one was five years old and then I worked a part-time job."

Her interactions with Zhou were limited but she came away with impressions:

> I think Zhou, like most Chinese, came to this country for a better life. In China, I think he was a farmer. He came from a small village far away from the city. In China, the water is not clean so many people carry hepatitis B and they don't know until they get sick from liver problems. His children stayed in China. He came over with his wife. He told me that he had been in the United States for a year [before their meeting at the ceremony]. He wasn't sick when he came here but after he got here, he felt sick and went to Mount Sinai [Hospital] to see the doctor and found out his liver is not working. I don't know if he got cancer or not.

Sau reported that she found Zhou's accent different from most Cantonese speakers. She suspected that was because he was from a remote village. "It was hard for me to understand him," she said. Presumably, Zhou might have experienced difficulty understanding Sau, as well. She recalled that he said to her—perhaps as a joke— "You are not a Chinese."

Sau said Zhou's wife did not come to the ceremony.

She told me on the phone, "I need the time to go to work." At the ceremony, Zhou went up to Michael's grandmother and bowed several times, saying [in English] "Thank you." In Chinese way, bowing is very respectful. He told me he had problems. I don't know what kind of problems. I really don't know his financials. He told me he and his wife lived in a very small place in Brooklyn.

. . . I told him I was a liver transplant recipient. He didn't say anything. I would say he is very lucky [to get the transplant].

. . . I think he just came to this country. Everything was new to him. He was a little bit nervous. He didn't seem interested. I think he thinks about how he can survive in this country. Mostly, he was quiet. He did not seem like a happy person.

. . . When he came to the US, I think he had no job. I think his wife worked. I think he does have a green card [which would have enabled him to work legally in the US].

Given her belief that Zhou had a Green Card, she expressed surprise when she learned that Zhou had not seen his doctor in a few years and that he may have returned to China. She did not have any contact information for him.

Still a volunteer at LiveOnNY, Sau is active and grateful. "I was fifty-three when I received my liver," she said. "I am now seventy-one. My health . . . so far so good. You get older and your body is sometimes a little bit worn, but I can walk. I can eat. I can talk. That's good."

DIRECTOR OF COMMUNICATIONS (RETIRED), LiveOnNY

J ulia Rivera's passion for organ transplantation began with the death of a young firefighter. She was working in the department of public relations and community affairs at Lincoln Hospital (a trauma center) in the Bronx when the firefighter was brought into the emergency room. "He was an extraordinary young man," she said of the firefighter. Julia described him further:

> He collected toys at Christmas and gave them out at different hospitals and community centers to poor kids. He came from an Irish family and was one of twelve children. I was called when he was brought in. Any time there was a major emergency, I was brought in. The media is all over the place when a first responder is injured or dies. And when one of their own is hurt, firefighters come together. His entire family was involved, too. They were a large, beautiful, very Catholic family committed to serving others. This was my first real, up close and personal experience

with organ donation because this young man's family decided to donate his organs. It was a powerful, moving experience for me.

After that I served on the ethics committee at Lincoln and became more familiar with organ donation. I met people who were transplant recipients, who had been touched by organ donation. I became aware, informed, and engaged with the donor families and the entire field of organ donation."

Born in Adjuntas, a small town in the central mountain range of Puerto Rico, Julia came to the United States when she was three and grew up in the Lower East Side of New York City. Later, her family moved to Brooklyn where she went to high school. "But the Lower East Side is really my home," she said.

In large part inspired by her experience with the young firefighter, after leaving Lincoln she began working at the New York Donor Network (later renamed LiveOnNY). At sixty-seven years old, she retired after working for LiveOnNY for eighteen years. "It was probably the most rewarding job of my career," she said.

Initially, she performed outreach to the Hispanic community. After a year, she became a public and professional education specialist and later was promoted to director of public relations which became director of communications. "My job was to educate the entire community about organ donation," she said. "I can talk in front of people and I'm pretty persuasive, but when a recipient or donor family member speaks—that moves the audience. They talk about their own experience."

LiveOnNY's service area includes the five boroughs of New York City, all of Long Island, some counties north of the Bronx, and Pike County in Pennsylvania. During her tenure, the department of communications grew from a staff of three to ten. Among others, she worked with religious leaders and elected officials. One of those was James Conte, a state legislator from Long Island who was an organ recipient. "He became a strong advocate for organ donation and he galvanized his fellow legislators," Julia said. During her tenure as the director of communications, in collaboration with fellow staff, other recovery organizations, and elected officials, the New York Donor Registry was created. "It made it easier to sign up to become a donor so when the time comes, the family knows what the donor's wishes are. Oftentimes, people don't talk about donations because it brings up cultural issues, myths, and misconceptions. One of those is 'If I talk about it, I'm gonna die next week.' The basic message is 'Donation is good. Donation is important. And it's important to discuss it with your family,' she said.

Julia also oversaw donor family services, and said the work was close to her heart:

> It provided after-care services to families who lost someone and whose loved ones also became organ donors. With staff from our donor family services, I had the privilege to coordinate meetings between donor families and their recipients. One of those meetings was attended by Michael Bovill's mother, father, sisters, grandmother, and aunt as well as four of the recipients of Michael's organs: Roxanne Watson, Scott Taffet, Zhou Yuan Li, and Elijah Parker as well as relatives and friends of the recipients. The gathering took place on June 1, 2011 at 1 Penn Plaza in New York City. This is a tender time when donor families meet the recipients and the recipients meet each other. I was very much involved.

Even before her path intersected with the young firefighter at Lincoln Hospital and working at LiveOnNY, Julia had personal experiences with death and dying. "My younger brother was thirty-three when he died from AIDS," she said. "My husband was thirty-four when he was killed in the Lower East Side. At the time of my husband's death, I was pregnant with my son and my daughter was a year old. Death has touched me in a lot of different ways. Working with LiveOnNY gave me a different perspective of death." Julia emphasized the significance of what being an organ donor means:

> When someone dies, they can extend the amazing gift of life to someone who is in need of an organ to be able to move on with their lives. I witnessed many, many situations where a child or older teenager received the gift of life. They survived. This transformed the agony of their donor's family and the entire community that surrounds the donor. When I met the family of the amazing firefighter and many other families, it meant for them that a horrible disaster did not have to be the end-all. That their loved one's death was not in vain. Because out of that death came somebody's life. It gave me a deeper appreciation of how vulnerable life is, how short it is, and how amazing it is that we can actually recycle our own bodies. We can make somebody else live longer. I had the privilege to meet people who have received an organ, gotten married, and had children. The lives of donor families are changed forever. It changes in such an amazing way—for good. It's a blessing. There are so many mysteries in life that can't be explained. The fact that this miracle of life breeds life in the middle of somebody else's death is . . . how do you explain that? It was a blessing to be there.

Julia is signed up to be an organ donor. "So is my entire family," she said. "My sister held out for the longest time and then three years ago, she said, 'You know, Julie, you're right. I'm going to be cremated so why should those organs go to waste?'" Julia happily reported that her sister signed up to be an organ donor.

DONNA BLOOMBERG

ONE OF MICHAEL'S TRANSPLANT COORDINATORS

A successful transplant coordinator possesses medical expertise; the vision and communication skills of the choreographer of a large dance ensemble; the outer and inner calmness of a beekeeper and belief in the sacredness of life and the goodness of organ transplants. Combine this unique skill set with the enormous tensions of a job that transcends life and death—the career span of most transplant coordinators is brief. Donna Bloomberg's more than eighteen years as a transplant coordinator for LiveOnNY is an exception.

"I knew pretty early on that nursing was right for me," she said. "It was just something I felt. Not one medical person in my working-class family. I was seventeen when I started nursing school."

Straight out of nursing school, Donna worked as a critical care nurse in an ICU for seven years. "It was quite a jump to go from nursing school to critical care. At the time, there was a huge nursing shortage. I wound up loving critical care and making a real difference," she said.

"In the ICU, I saw transplant coordinators come in to evaluate potential organ donors. It was interesting and seemed to me to be an intriguing job for a nurse. I loved the concept of organ donation and all that it meant. To me, this was making the ultimate difference. It felt like it was my calling."

Her "calling" as a transplant coordinator requires the navigation of powerful emotions, family dynamics, religious practices, remarkable technology, and medical interventions. "Unfortunately, someone has passed on, but you can still make a difference so that multiple people don't have to die," Donna said. "Working to help others live on. . . it was just amazing to me. I applied for a job with the New York Organ Donors Network and was hired."

Donna's job is to go into different hospitals to evaluate the viability of potential candidates for organ donation. If the person is a viable candidate, she enlists the help of staff from LiveOnNY's Family Counseling Department who speak with the family to request their consent for organ donation. "My job is to clinically manage the donor and to maximize organ function," she said, "so that the recipient is receiving the best quality organ possible and potentially providing the best possible outcome after transplant." She further described her role:

> To clinically manage the donor means optimizing their organ function. When you're brain dead, you've lost a lot of your hormonal balance to maintain function of your organs. It is a matter of time before the body catches up to where your brain is and body function shuts down. It's my job to keep that at bay until the transplant happens. I'm monitoring blood levels, blood pressure, vital signs, hemodynamic status [the ability to keep temperature and heart rate stable]. I don't prescribe medication. As a nurse, I'm not licensed to do that. We work with the critical care teams in the hospital to formulate a collaborative plan of care for the donor.

She also coordinates the organ recovery teams. Depending on the number of organs to be recovered for transplant, there may be from one to seven recovery teams involved. "The whole job is a pretty huge multifaceted task. It's intense at times and it's the best thing I've ever done," she said.

The time between the family giving their consent for organ donation to the actual recovery of organs depends on the family. Donna estimates that in most cases this is thirty-six to forty-eight hours. "The families are going through the worst period of their lives," she said. There are a number of questions she asks herself when first interacting with the family of the organ donor:

> *Are they accepting the death or are they not? Are they ready to donate or are they not? Do they have time constraints or do they not? It takes a certain personality to coordinate this and have everybody stay calm in the process—and that has to happen. You need to know when there's flexibility in a situation and when there's not. You need adherence to your commitment. If you make a commitment to a family that this process is going to happen within thirty-six hours, you need to make it happen within thirty-six hours."*

> *For the most part, there is not a lot of tension. Families are allowed to stay with the donor until they are wheeled into the OR. Some families opt to stay until the very end and will walk with the donor to the OR. In most cases, however, families will pick a time to say goodbye. Some will have a religious service if their religious beliefs entail that. We work very hard to be as unobtrusive as possible in their last hours with their family member.*

Donna believes in the mission of LiveOnNY. "It's my belief inside, as well. Without that internal commitment, I couldn't do it. I enjoy making a difference. Once a family makes the decision to donate, it is my job to make that happen . . . and make their gift mean something," she said.

When asked if a sense of humor is involved with her work, Donna said, "Not for me."

The transplant coordinator communicates with surgeons and physicians caring for potential organ recipients, schedules the recovery surgery, secures the necessary facilities, and choreographs the surgical recovery process. Multiple recovery teams usually arrive at the OR together.

> If a heart is going to Columbia Presbyterian [in New York City] and the lungs are going to Duke University in North Carolina, the Duke team will fly in. The Columbia Presbyterian team will usually take an ambulance. Everyone is in the OR at the same time. We start with a time-out where we make sure that every single person in the room is on board with the procedure, who is responsible for what, and then we do a moment of silence in dedication to the donor's life. Everyone in the OR participates. The recovery is a surgical procedure, not unlike many surgical procedures. Organs are recovered. The body is always treated with the utmost respect.
>
> I am the facilitator of this. It is a powerful and amazing job—one that transcends the boundaries of traditional nursing. It's so amazing. I've been here for eighteen years and I wouldn't be anywhere else. It's just as powerful today as the day I started.

During the recovery process for Michael's organs, there were five separate recovery teams composed of approximately twenty-five medical personnel in the OR at the same time. "We rely on collaboration between the recovery teams," Donna said.

> You may have a situation where one of the teams has a recipient who is not doing well and they may need to get back to their OR faster. Another team might wait three or four hours. There's a huge amount of respect between the teams and us. Everyone

involved in this process has this understanding and respect for each other and the process as a whole. It's what amazes me so much about this job—there exists so much collaboration between so many people to make this happen.

Donna was with Michael one time when he was hospitalized. She reported, "It was for a few hours late at night. At the time I was there, he didn't meet all the criteria for brain death. So, he needed to be reevaluated, and I was there to update things. And then the case was taken over by someone else."

Reflecting on eighteen years as a transplant coordinator, Donna compared her long tenure with that of other transplant coordinators. "The average time someone is a coordinator is pretty limited," she said. "The career span for coordinators at LiveOnNY is longer than the national average. It's a great place to work. The company as a whole really cares about its employees. Some things and personnel have changed over the years but the one thing that hasn't changed is how I've been treated. They are like a family to me and my colleagues."

Donna expressed that every day is different when working as a transplant coordinator:

I can't speak to what others feel but this work is not routine for me. I experience awe, magic, beauty, and love in every case. I see and interact with the families. I'm not just in the OR. Every patient that I take to the OR has a mother or a father or a sister or a brother who they are leaving. And for every family that is the hardest day in their lives. I am there to hopefully make it a little bit better for them if that is possible. Over the years, my work has been incorporated into my own life. Nothing will show you that life is fragile like this job. Every one of us can lose our life tomorrow. It has made me appreciate that in my own life and my children's lives.

Donna is the mother of two children. Her daughter is enrolled in nursing school. "She doesn't think I had a role in her decision," Donna said, "but I'm happy she decided to become a nurse."

When asked if she is signed up to be an organ donor, Donna emphatically responded, "Oh my god yes, I'm signed up. And both my children, as well. Totally on their own."

Despite the demands of the job, Donna felt that she found her calling in life:

> There's a place for everybody in this world. If you find your place, it makes for a pretty amazing life. Why did I see the coordinators walk into the ICU? Why did I grab onto it? I don't know. The journey puts many forks in the road. I don't know what brought me to this, but it's the right place. I will probably end my career as a transplant coordinator.

KAREN GANS

ONE OF MICHAEL'S TRANSPLANT COORDINATORS

I n her work as a transplant coordinator, the primary person Karen Gans interacts with has been declared brain dead or is likely to be declared brain dead very soon. When Karen first meets a candidate for organ donation, he or she is almost always verbally unresponsive. "I always talk to the donor," she said.

Even if they're brain dead, it doesn't mean that you can't talk to them. Their heart is still beating. I always introduce myself. Their family is still there and they talk to them. It's not dead like they're in the ground. They're still there. As a nurse, you're trained to always introduce yourself. It's respectful. This work is a very humbling experience. I do experience the presence of that person's soul. I do feel a connection with the donor. The connection goes away once the organ recovery process is finished. That's when I say goodbye to the donor. Before that, they're still there and I'm still caring for them. We still honor them. Even though they're brain dead, they're still human.

Karen grew up in Canada where she graduated from nursing school in 1996. "As a senior in high school, I decided nursing was the job I wanted. I stuck with it ever since. I enjoy caring for people. Nursing is a trusted profession. There were nurses in my family, too," she said.

Because there were few available nursing jobs in Canada when she graduated, she accepted a position in the ICU at a hospital in Texas. "It was a big jump to go from nursing school to critical care, but I had six months of excellent training and was well-prepared," she said. Karen worked as a critical care nurse in the ICU for ten years when she was recruited by a visiting transplant coordinator. "The coordinator who recruited me knew everything about the donor. I wanted to be like that," she said. In 2006, Karen began working for the New York Organ Donors Network (later LiveOnNY) where she continues to be passionately employed. "I like the autonomy of being a transplant coordinator. You're doing everything for this donor."

Her job involves responding to area hospitals when a potential organ donor is identified. "When I'm going to the hospital for the first time to evaluate a potential donor, I definitely prepare myself for what I might encounter," she said. She credited her training for enabling her to become a thorough, prepared nurse:

> As coordinators, we're taught to expect everything. We think about the case. We think about what potentially could be going on with the donor and the donor family. How are they doing? Are they accepting everything that's going on? How stable is the donor? What kind of culture is it in the hospital? It's like you're mentally preparing yourself for the big game. You have to psych yourself up. We have a lot to think about. People's lives are involved. Families are involved. This is somebody's brother, sister, mother, or father or child. It's not just the technical

aspect of things. There are a lot of intense feelings involved, too. You have to think about that when you go into a hospital. The hospital staff might be upset because they weren't able to save this patient. There's a lot we have to be prepared for when we respond to our cases.

We try to make donation a seamless process. It's not just a job. It's kind of like your life. You live and breathe it. When alerted to a potential donor, we work with that patient's medical team, the hospital administrator, and nursing team. We make sure that if they haven't gotten to the point of consent [receiving formal consent from the donor's family for the donor's organs to be removed for transplant], that they maintain the patient up until they do or don't become a donor. We ask the medical team, "Can you maintain the patient so that they can become a donor?"

The determination of legal brain death is a complex medical process with enormous implications. Brain death (sometimes referred to as "death by neurologic criteria") is determined by a rigorous series of tests. (Excerpts of the Guidelines for Determining Brain Death from the New York State Department of Health are found at the end of this chapter.) The tests determine whether basic brain stem reflexes are or are not intact. These include:

1. Corneal reflex (sometimes referred to as the blink reflex—an involuntary blinking of the eyelids caused by stimulation of the cornea)

2. Pupillary response (whether the pupils dilate or are fixed)

3. Oculocephalic reflex (moving the head to determine if the eyes respond to that movement)

4. Caloric reflex test (ice water placed in ear to determine if the eyes respond)

5. Tracheal response (sometimes referred to as cough

response—tested by inhaling treated air to determine function of the respiratory tract)

6. Pharyngeal response (sometimes referred to as gag response—testing for the gag reflex by touching multiple locations in the back of the throat)

To be legally declared "dead by neurologic criteria," the patient must not have any of these reflexes functioning. If one of the reflex tests is positive and the others are negative, that person is not considered brain dead. Assuming negative responses for all six tests, confirmatory tests are then administered when patient is taken off the ventilator for ten minutes with multiple associated tests and negative results required for final determination of brain death.

Karen stressed that there is a difference between "unresponsive" and "brain dead." "Brain death means the patient is not coming back," she said. "Being unresponsive may mean that some reflexes are still intact. This can become a delicate issue for the families of the potential donors. It requires members of the medical team to explain the difference."

Karen operates in the literal world of life and death; the patient; the patient's family; medical staff of the hospital; and physicians and surgeons of the recovery teams. This is a realm where tension and anxiety could be crippling. Not so for Karen: "I never approach work with anxiety. I'm one of the calmest coordinators out there. I'm able to roll with the punches and be a calm voice to people—be it family, or hospital staff, or other coordinators. I appreciate being that person to other people."

This ability to remain calm in the midst of the dramas unfolding around her has enabled Karen to function effectively for more than ten years as a transplant coordinator. "I think most coordinators last three to four years before moving on," she said.

I love what I do. I enjoy what I do. I work for a great company that respects me. They take care of me. Being a transplant coordinator is not the easiest thing to do because you work twenty-four-hour shifts. I have trouble picturing myself working twenty-four-hour shifts when I'm fifty-five... In the future, I'd like to stay in the world of transplant, but not necessarily work twenty-four hours straight as a transplant coordinator.

I try to separate work from home. When I'm not working, I spend time with my husband and my kids. We do a lot of things together as a family. Personally, I love to garden. During the growing season, I'm outside a lot. I talk to my fruits and vegetables and they have to talk back to me [laughs]. It's very calming to me.

Karen was the first transplant coordinator from LiveOnNY to see Michael after his accident.

There was a lot of family there. I did the initial evaluation and worked with the medical team at his hospital. I remember feeling sad that he was a young guy. You see the family and feel saddened by it. I did not interact with his family because it was too early in the process. The hospital staff was actively treating him. His condition was very unstable at the time. He was being maintained with IV drip to maintain his blood pressure. They thought he was brain dead, but he was still taking some respirations [breathing] so he was sent to the OR in an attempt to save him.

During that procedure, three hundred cubic centimeters of blood were removed from Michael's brain. This took place on Monday, July 12, 2010, about thirty-six hours after his accident which occurred late on Saturday night, July 10th. On July 13th, he was taken for a nuclear medicine study which showed that he still had some flow to his brain. On the 14th, another study was conducted and found that he was brain dead. He was legally declared brain dead on the 15th. His organs were recovered on the 16th. The recovery process began just before four o'clock. It was completed at nine thirty that evening. On the 17th, his lungs, heart, kidneys, and liver were successfully transplanted into five recipients hospitalized in New York City.

"With Michael—who was a trauma victim—we worked with the medical team to maintain his stability," she said. "That's because if a trauma victim passes away before we get consent, we'd never have any organ donors. Sometimes, trauma patients are really unstable."

Karen outlined her role in the transplant process:

As a transplant coordinator, I am the one coordinating the [organ] recovery. We bring the donor to the OR where the recovery teams converge. They are out of sight of the family out of respect. Just outside the OR will be the last time the family will see the donor before they see him at the morgue. The surgeons are very respectful of this. Inside the OR, it is pretty calm. The surgeons are very respectful of everything that's going on. It's a very busy time. Each surgical team has its own job and needs. I maintain the clinical peace in there to make sure that nobody's being too loud and to make sure that everybody is on the same page. It's a whole bunch of people who can be new to each other, all doing the same thing. Transplant coordinators maintain respect for the donor and make sure that everything goes smoothly. There's a lot of different personalities in the OR and I've never really encountered any conflict because all the surgical teams know we're all there for the same purpose.

Karen mediates a complex and crowded situation. "At Michael's recovery there were approximately twenty-five people in the OR. Usually, with multiple organs to be recovered, there are three to four surgeons working at the same time. Each team works exclusively on the organ they are recovering. It's very tight in there," she said.

She has worked as a nurse for half her life. "It's my calling. I really love doing it. I couldn't imagine doing anything else. From this work, I see that everything is just one. There's no divide. It's just one."

GUIDELINES FOR DETERMINING BRAIN DEATH

New York State Department of Health

November 2011

DEFINITION

New York State regulation defines brain death as the irreversible loss of all function of the brain, including the brain stem. . . The three essential findings in brain death are coma, absence of brain stem reflexes, and apnea. An evaluation for brain death should be considered in patients who have suffered a massive, irreversible brain injury of identifiable cause. A patient properly determined to be brain dead is legally and clinically dead.

The diagnosis of brain death is primarily clinical. No other tests are required if the full clinical examination, including an assessment of brain stem reflexes and an apnea test, is conclusively performed. In the absence of either complete clinical findings consistent with brain death or ancillary tests demonstrating brain death, brain death cannot be diagnosed.

CLINICAL ASSESSMENT OF BRAIN STEM REFLEXES

If an appropriate period of time has passed since the onset of the brain insult to exclude the possibility of recovery, one clinical assessment of brain function and an apnea test should be sufficient to pronounce brain death. Only after the possibility of recovery has been excluded should the brain function and apnea test be performed. However, if the possibility of recovery has not been excluded, these examinations should be deferred.

Note: Repeat brain death examinations are advisable before proceeding to an apnea test in young children.

In addition, for patients who are 18 years or older, normal core temperature (>36°C (98.8°F)) should be achieved, particularly in patients who have been hypothermic. In addition, normal systolic pressure (≥100 mm Hg) (option: mean arterial pressure ≥65 mm Hg) should be achieved before assessing brain stem reflexes.

Where these conditions are met, the following clinical indications verify the occurrence of brain death:

- **Coma:** No evidence of responsiveness. Eye opening or eye movement to noxious stimuli is absent. Noxious stimuli should not produce a motor response other than spinally mediated reflexes.

- **Absence of brain stem reflexes:**
  » Absence of pupillary response to bright light in both eyes. Usually the pupils are fixed in midsize or dilated position (4-9 mm).

  » Absence of ocular movements using oculocephalic testing (only when no fracture or instability of the cervical spine or skull base is apparent or may be suspected clinically) and oculovestibular reflex testing.

  » Absence of corneal reflexes.

  » Absence of facial muscle movement in response to a noxious stimulus.

  » Absence of pharyngeal (gag) and tracheal (cough) reflexes.

APNEA TEST

Generally, the apnea test is the final step in the determination of brain death, and is performed after establishing the irreversibility and unresponsiveness of coma, and the absence of brainstem reflexes.

Before performing the apnea test, the physician must determine that the patient meets the following conditions:

- Core temperature >36°C or 96.8°F.

- PaCO2 35-45 mm Hg.

- Normal PaO2. Option: pre-oxygenation for at least 10 minutes with 100% oxygen to PaO2 >200 mm Hg.

- Normotension. Adjust fluids and (if necessary) vasopressors to a systolic blood pressure ≥100 mm Hg (option: mean arterial pressure ≥65 mm Hg).

After determining that the patient meets the prerequisites above, the physician should conduct the apnea test as follows:

- Connect a pulse oximeter.

- Disconnect the ventilator.

  » Apnea can be assessed reliably only by disconnecting the ventilator, as the ventilator can sense small changes in tubing pressure and provide a breath that could suggest breathing effort by the patient where none exists.

- Deliver 100% O2, 6 L/min by placing a catheter through the endotracheal tube and close to the level of the carina. Option: use a T-piece with 10 cm H2O CPAP and deliver 100% O2, 12 L/min.

- Draw a baseline arterial blood gas.

- Look closely for respiratory movements (abdominal or chest excursions that produce adequate tidal volumes) for 8-10 minutes.

- Measure PaO2, PaCO2, and pH after approximately 8-10 minutes and reconnect the ventilator.

- If respiratory movements are absent and PaCO2 is ≥60 mm Hg (*option:* 20 mm Hg increase in PaCO2 over a baseline normal PaCO2), the apnea test supports the diagnosis of brain death.

- If respiratory movements are observed, the apnea test result is negative (*i.e.*, does not support the diagnosis of brain death).

- Connect the ventilator if, during testing, the systolic blood pressure becomes <90 mm Hg (or below age-appropriate thresholds in children less than 18 years of age) or the pulse oximeter indicates significant oxygen desaturation (<85% for >30 seconds), or cardiac arrhythmias develop; immediately draw an arterial blood sample and analyze arterial blood gas. If $PaCO_2$ is ≥60 mm Hg or $PaCO_2$ increase is ≥20 mm Hg over baseline normal $PaCO_2$, the apnea test result supports the diagnosis of brain death; if $PaCO_2$ is <60 mm Hg and $PaCO_2$ increase is <20 mm Hg over baseline normal $PaCO_2$, the result is indeterminate. If adequate blood pressure and oxygenation can be maintained, the apnea test can be repeated for a longer period of time (10-15 minutes) or an ancillary test can be considered if the result is indeterminate.

DISCONTINUE CARDIO-RESPIRATORY SUPPORT IN ACCORDANCE WITH HOSPITAL POLICIES, INCLUDING THOSE FOR ORGAN DONATION

When a patient is certified as brain dead and the ventilator is to be discontinued, the family should be treated with sensitivity and respect. If family members wish, they may be offered the opportunity to attend while the ventilator is discontinued. However, family members should be prepared for the possibly disturbing clinical activity that they may witness. When organ donation is contemplated, ventilatory support will conclude in the operating room and family attendance is not appropriate.

PART TWO

RELIGIOUS/SPIRITUAL PERSPECTIVES ON TRANSPLANTS

FATHER ALOYSIUS THUMMA

CATHOLIC PRIEST & HEART TRANSPLANT RECIPIENT

A CATHOLIC PERSPECTIVE ON TRANSPLANTS

W hile I was writing *Michael's Legacy*, a long-brewing, moderately uncomfortable relationship escalated into a very uncomfortable one. "Mary," the person with whom I was experiencing this discomfort, and I frequently crossed paths in the course of our lives. These intersections were unavoidable unless one of us chose to change significant circumstances of our day-to-day existences. I believe I am telling the truth when I say that I had largely succeeded in recognizing that the discomfort was my experience and not turning Mary into a villain. With my wife's encouragement, I practiced a loving meditation for Mary and her wellbeing. I followed the advice of the Buddhist monk Thich Nhat Hanh of breathing mindfully and working to transform the discomfort into a peaceful equanimity. Still, I allowed my discomfort with Mary and her actions to "get on my nerves" and "get under my skin"—not healthy places for this sensation to take up residence.

It was in the middle one of my rough patches with Mary that I spoke with Father Aloysius Thumma Gnana Prakash, a Catholic priest who received a heart transplant at the age of sixty. It was at this time that I began interviewing clergy of many faith traditions to learn about their unique perspectives on organ donation and transplant.

In my work, I call individuals to whom I am a total unknown and stranger, tell them what I'm working on, and ask if they'd be willing for me to interview them. It's surprising to me how willing many people are to me as a stranger and agree to share their time and tell their stories.

On the phone, Father Aloysius was warm and receptive. He spoke English fluently with a strong Indian accent. I loved his voice. When he heard that if it was more convenient and comfortable for him we could have the interview by phone, he immediately indicated he preferred we meet at his parish home in Katonah, New York. Enveloped by his warmth, I readily accepted driving across the Hudson River and up the Taconic Thruway, something that typically I would have avoided. I wanted to be in his presence.

During the drive, I recognized my discomfort with the situation with Mary was active. Despite my efforts to drive mindfully, I allowed the discomfort to take hold.

I arrived at the parish home, rang the doorbell, and was immediately greeted by a trim man wearing a priest's white collar. Father Aloysius invited me into the spare but warm dining room. He asked, "Are you a coffee man or a tea man?" He scooted off to the kitchen to brew a cup of tea for me and returned with cookies on the side. I felt genuinely welcomed. As I was setting up my recording devices (I use two, in case one fails), he said, "Before we begin the interview, tell me about yourself." I am in the business of interviewing others, not the other way around. I sensed this man wanted to meet me, know me perhaps as much as I wanted to hear his story.

After I shared a bit about my life, I thought we were ready for the "real" interview to begin. But before that, Father Aloysius asked me about how I came to be writing this particular book. I felt waves of warmth from this man who appeared to be totally invested in meeting me. I told him in some detail how I met Roxanne Watson and became more and more interested in Michael's story and the stories of people who intersected with Michael and his legacy. Father Aloysius listened with full attention. Then he was ready for me to ask him questions.

As he spoke, I recognized my discomfort with Mary dissipating and then disappearing. Father Aloysius' rendering of his life story was so filled with goodness, love, and service that I became free of anything other than a peaceful calm.

Usually when an interview is done and I'm about to leave, I shake hands with the person I just interviewed. At the threshold to the parish house, after we shook hands, Father Aloysius opened the door to let me out. I turned to him and said, "I'd like a hug." Certainly, not a professional gesture or statement. It would have been more honest for me to say, "I am moved and inspired by you and your work and would welcome a hug. A hug from you would be healing to me." Father Aloysius gave me a warm hug. I felt I was in the presence of a holy man.

The effects of his embrace still resonate with me. From that hug and time with Father Aloysius, I can honestly say that my feelings towards Mary softened.

After waiting— for a heart or to die—in intensive care for three months, Father Aloysius Thumma's cardiologist informed him that his new heart would arrive in three or four hours. Because his heart was so weak, Father Aloysius knew that without a successful transplant, death was imminent. "During those three months, I understood that if I left the hospital, I wouldn't have stayed alive," he said.

As medical staff prepared him for major surgery, Father Aloysius remembers the anesthesiologist asking him, "Why are you so cheerful? You're not afraid?"

Father Aloysius answered, "My suffering will end today. If the transplant is successful, all my pain will end. If it doesn't work, I'll be dead and all my pain will end. So, my suffering will end from this moment onwards. I am so happy."

Father Aloysius was born in 1951 in India. His parents were Catholic. "The part of India where I come from is two percent Catholic," he said. "The village where I grew up was predominantly Catholic." Religion has been an integral part of his life ever since he was a young boy:

My parents were not very educated. They were farmers. They were very religious. We were six children. My parents always looked at life from the religious perspective. From them I picked up religion in a personal way. As I grew up and when I was in college, the question came up, "What do I want to be?" I had a very good example of a parish priest. My pastor was a very enlightened man. He was a simple man. He started a school. At times, he did not have much to eat because he sacrificed himself to the school and parish. To me, he was heroic. And I chose to follow his example. My formation [training] was a long process— eleven years. I was ordained in 1980. I have been a priest now for thirty-eight years. I didn't mind being celibate, not being married.

Four years after his ordination, the bishop's conference of his region asked Father Aloysius to go to Rome for advanced studies of spirituality and counseling. The intention was that after completion of these studies, he would return and teach at the seminary, which he did for four years. Then his diocese sent him to the United States for additional study to further enhance his teaching.

"I came to the United States in 1997," he said. He continued:

In 1999, I had a heart attack. My heart was very damaged. Thirty-eight percent of my heart was paralyzed. The doctors said it could stop at any time. To help me, they implanted a cardiac nuclear element to supplement the energy of my heart. It was powered by nuclear energy. After five years, the device was getting weaker. At that time, a new device called a cardiac nuclear defibrillator was implanted. Because my heart was stopping so often, I was getting a lot of shocks from the defibrillator. With each shock, my heart was weakened. Eventually, I was so weak, I collapsed and was brought to the hospital. Doctors tested me for three days and then reported, "There is no option. You are going to die." But one doctor, Dr. Manish Parikh, came back to me. He said, "You do have an option. You could receive a heart transplant if you get the right heart and in time." So I said, "Yes, why not?"

There was testing of every part of my body. Checking to make sure that my health insurance was adequate. They said, "Yes, go ahead." Then we had to contact the cardinal's office here. They said, "Yes." Then I had to contact my bishop back at home [India] and he said yes. All the medical tests came back with encouraging results. I never used drugs or smoked or drank alcohol.

The transplant team expressed concern that Father Aloysius did not have the support system to care for him after a heart transplant.

They said to me, "You don't have anybody here to care for you after the transplant. You have no family here. You will need a lot of moral and physical support."

I called the parish. I was in the Bronx at the time at Our Lady of the Assumption Church in Pelham Bay. We had very devoted people there. I said Holy Mass every morning for the nuns. The Mother Superior said, "I will stand by you [to provide care after the transplant]." One of our volunteers said, "I will support Father." They both signed the papers provided by the transplant team committing to care for me.

With all this in place, Father Aloysius entered intensive care at Columbia Presbyterian Hospital to wait for the right heart . . . and to make sure he stayed alive until the right heart was available. "With the technology and staff, they were able to keep me alive," he reported.

I was in intensive care for three months waiting for a heart. My heart was so weak, I felt a lot of pain, especially when I got shocks in my chest [from the defibrillator]. I had no enthusiasm. I was on high doses of medication. Life was dull. My feet would swell. I was unable to drive. I knew I was coming to the end. I was never fearful. Fear never entered into my life. I don't remember getting depressed or anxious.

During his three months in intensive care, Father Aloysius came to appreciate the American medical system:

I didn't have anyone close to me to check on me or my doctors. The medical people were so dedicated. In three months, I never remember one doctor or one nurse who neglected me. They did their jobs perfectly. Not as a job. They did it as a devotion. I took that as a priest, as a Christian, in the Judeo-Christian spirit, as self-giving love. I noticed this in every doctor, every nurse. It was always their patients came first. I don't think they were aware of their hunger or thirst.

When he was told that a heart was on the way, there was a flurry of preparations and then he was put to sleep. The following evening, his previous pastor and close friend, Monsignor Donald Dwyer, took the unconscious Father Aloysius' hand and shouted,

"Father Aloysius! Father Aloysius! You had a successful operation!"

"I remember hearing his voice as if it was far away," said Father Aloysius. "And I remember squeezing his hand. The next morning, I got up. I had a very good appetite. The nurse asked me what I wanted to eat. I said, 'I would like to eat a plateful of chicken curry.' She brought it to me. I ate. Soon, I was walking through the hospital."

From the time of his first heart attack leading up to the transplant, Father Aloysius had undergone multiple medical procedures and endured many electrical shocks to his heart from the implanted defibrillator. This had caused significant damage to his heart and chest that led to post-operative complications causing him to hiccough day and night. A second operation successfully repaired and cleaned up the old damage. Two weeks later he was discharged.

"Before I was discharged," he said, "the doctors told me I must go to rehab." His colleagues, however, had another plan in mind:

The nuns said, "No, we don't send our priest to rehab. We will rehab him at the convent where we have a dispensary." The sisters, they know what they're doing. They put me in their guest room and nursed me. After six weeks, I was celebrating Mass. I am a good cook and they wanted me to cook whatever I wanted in their kitchen. I cooked and I ate and after six weeks I went back to work full-time in my parish. No complications. I had lost forty pounds when I was in intensive care and I regained twenty-five pounds. The doctors said, "You don't need any more weight." So for the last six years, my weight is the same, 142 pounds.

At the time of the transplant, Father Aloysius was sixty years old. His donor was twenty. "My heart is very young," he said.

Much younger than the rest of me. In a few weeks, I will be sixty-seven. My heart will be twenty-seven. In myself, today, I see physical energy. I find myself climbing a tree. That energy, that inclination is there. Before the transplant, I did not have a short temper. Suddenly expressing my anger was not in my character. In the last six years, two times, I've irrationally expressed my anger. I'm very conscious of these two incidents. That gesture was not in my nature before the transplant.

About my donor, I know this. My heart came from Cincinnati, Ohio. My donor was a very sporty young man. He used to go on snowmobiles. He had an accident. He went into the air, twisting the vehicle. It fell on him. He was brain dead. I feel that he loved life and he wanted to help others because he signed up to be an organ donor through his driver's license.

Father Aloysius and his donor's parents have exchanged letters. They don't contact each other directly. Each sent their letters to the New York Organ Donor Network which forwards them.

I've told them, "I am a Catholic priest. My community will be very happy to meet you. You are welcome." Initially, they expressed their wish to visit me and I wanted very much to meet them. But since then, I never received another letter expressing their wish to visit me. Maybe they are shy. I don't know. I am not forcing them or pressuring them. Maybe one day they will visit.

I am absolutely grateful. Every day, I think of them. I pray for them. His parents had two children one boy, one girl. When the boy died, he was expecting to be godfather to his niece who was coming into the world. Just a couple of weeks before she was born, he died. That was a grave shock for his parents.

"I still imagine him holding a little baby, his little niece, his goddaughter. That makes me to want cry. It gives me a great kick to think—because I carry his heart—that I am godfather to that child. She would be almost six years old now."

I want to see that family. It would be a great thing for me. I want to have dinner with them. I want to have a great time with them. Both of my parents are dead. Two of my brothers and one of my sisters have died. But somehow, though I never saw them, I have such a strong spiritual feeling for my donor's family. In my half-sleep I think of them. I am deeply connected to them. In my prayers, they come to my mind.

I don't have a photograph of my donor. But I always imagine—this is a fantasy—that he was a very strong guy. because I eat a lot of food and I don't gain weight. Before, I was not a great eater but since the transplant, I eat a good amount of food more than I did before. I don't know if he had a sense of humor.

I imagine my donor an as a nineteen year old and he gets the thought to donate his organs if he dies. To have such a great culture of selfless love planted in his young heart . . . My philosophy is this: selfless love is the way of my life—the only thing to do with my life. Christ is selfless love. And at the age of nineteen, when he took his driver's license [when he signed up to be an organ donor], he already knew that. I strongly believe that he was Christian. I don't know, but I strongly believe he was. Even Jewish, because Jewish faith is selfless love. And we Christians have a Jewish background. As Christ said, "I came not to destroy it [Judaism] but to make it more fulfilled."

The transplant deepened my faith. I think science and religion should go together. God is truth. It has become clear to me through this operation. It is like in the lab, it is proved. Faith in God was always there in me. Faith in my fellow human beings is much deeper now. Faith is to look beyond what you comprehend. You know it is there, but you can't express it. Take for example, my doctor. Other doctors had told me there is no possibility for my survival. He came back to me and said, "There is a possibility." Why did he take such interest? I'm not his blood relation.

Father Aloysius cited two more examples of how his faith deepened during his illness:

The day I was rushed to the hospital, there was this doctor, a resident, a Jewish man. I asked him how many hours he was working. He said thirty-six. Thirty-six hours on duty. Even though I was in such pain and discomfort, I was watching him. Towards the end of his shift, I asked him, "How many hours did you sleep?" He said, "Hardly any." It says to me that this man's spirit is to reach out to the other. To make money, there are so many easy ways. You don't have to be a doctor and stand there for thirty-six hours.

After the transplant, I had this terrible case of hiccoughs. The nurse was supposed to leave me at seven o'clock in the morning. She had worked from seven in the evening the night before. But she stayed until nine o'clock. Because that night, I had complained a couple of times that I was so uncomfortable. Usually, I am not a man to complain, but I thought something was seriously wrong. And she recognized that, too. At seven in the morning another nurse came but she didn't leave me until nine o'clock. She didn't leave until she was sure that I would be fixed. Those two hours I was watching her, even though I was in pain, I wondered why she was staying. My faith in my fellow human beings is not so shallow now. I take everybody very seriously. That nurse staying with me until nine in the morning—she deepened my faith.

During his extended stay in intensive care, Father Aloysius observed how he handled the very real life and death experience compared with other patients.

I am not criticizing my fellow patients. I am reporting what I observed. They were not focused on their sickness. Very often,

they were focusing on other things . . . like twenty-four hour TV.
My experience was different. I never watched the TV. I never
read the newspaper. I never looked at my face. For three months,
I never looked at my face. I have such a great discipline that
I inherited.

When I was a candidate for the priesthood, I took a one-year
leave to discipline myself in a monastery with a Hindu sage.
His name was Dharmananda. Dharma means "law." Ananda
means "happiness." He was one of the disciples of Mahatma
Gandhi. In that year, I went through strict yoga discipline. Every
day, I made my one-hour shavasana. There are eighty-six asanas
[positions]. The final asana is a one-hour meditative practice of
shavasana. Translated from Sanskrit, it means "corpse pose." The
practitioner lies full-length on their back in the position of a corpse.

You focus on what is happening to your body. You go through
your bones, how your body is dissolving into elements of the earth.
It gives you a realistic sense of your life. It gives focus and reality.
I used this yogic teaching and practice when I was in intensive care.

Born and growing up in India, having studied, lived, and
worked in Europe and the United States gives Father Aloysius
a unique perspective on humanity. "Everyone wants to live for
something beyond themselves," he said. "They want to live for
something. I strongly feel this. And as the United States was built
on the Judeo-Christian culture, I believe culturally the people of
the United States are deeply focused on the other. I was born in
India, in a different culture. In India, things are a little different
philosophically. If something happens, it is your *maya*, your karma,
your fate."

As a Catholic priest and recipient of a heart transplant, Father
Aloysius reflected on the Catholic belief regarding organ donations
and transplants. "The church is very clear about transplants. We
mention it in our prayers. It is a part of our liturgy. We teach about

it. I frequently ask people to consider becoming organ donors. This is something I want to promote. I do it whenever I have the chance. The Catholic church is very much in favor of the transplant."

Yet, brain transplants specifically spark a different conversation:

It is a great question for me what I would think if brains were able to be transplanted. If I am carrying your brain, I'm sure I am carrying all your memories, all your emotional baggage, history. I am not sure that this is a good idea. I think that when people talk about the heart being the embodiment of the soul, it is meant symbolically. Science teaches us that it is the brain that starts to grow even before the heart. We see some habit of the grandpa in the grandchild. We see some gene from the heart working through the brain. As Catholics, we have a different meaning of "symbol." A symbol signifies what is inexpressible. For example, when we say the body of Jesus Christ in the Eucharist, is a great symbol for us, a sacramental symbol.

And then comes a strong faith. My Catholic faith. That death is not the permanent end. There is life after death. That joy can only come from God. I have that joy. On the eighth of March, 1999, when I had a heart attack, I was nearly in the death. I knew how the soul can merge with God. Even with the pain of the heart attack. That pain is terrible. It feels as if you put this plank on my chest and pile six people on that plank crushing me. That is the pain I experienced. In that pain, I'm almost dying, but I can see the happiness. That memory is still great. That God's grace is there for me. My faith is confirmed. There is happiness into the death. And thank God for the medicine that unblocked the blocked veins and I survived.

Father Aloysius received his new heart on the day Catholics celebrate the conversion of St. Paul. That holiday recognizes the change of heart St. Paul experienced when he accepted Jesus as the Savior. Father Aloysius explained:

Paul was a very determined young man. He was a very orthodox Jew and he was determined to kill all the Christians because he was convinced that God is one, and that this fanatic named Jesus claims to be God, and that all these people believing in Jesus should be put to death. Paul is on his way to Damascus when he is struck down and blinded. He is instructed to go to a certain location in Damascus and remain there and a messenger will come. Paul obeys. On the third day, Paul was still blind and the messenger sent by Jesus arrives. The messenger restores Paul's sight and teaches him about Jesus Christ. Paul is a changed man and proclaims that Jesus is the promised one identified in the Old Testament. He became a powerful teacher. Before this day, Paul's name had been Saul. He became Paul on this day of his conversion. On the day we celebrate Paul's conversion, Saul became Paul. On the day I received my donor's heart, a part of me became my donor's self. When I was studying for the priesthood, St. Paul was one my favorite saints. He was a determined man. He believed that Judaism is the only truth and that everything else is false. But once he realized that Jesus is the Savior, he was very determined to spread that word in a very non-violent way. He died very well in death, praising the Lord. It is meaningful to me that I received my heart on this day of St. Paul's change of heart.

Father Aloysius's complete family name is Thumma Gnana Prakash. *Thumma* is a strong tree that farmers use to make plows. The tree can withstand heat and drought and is long-lived. *Gnana* is wisdom. *Prakash* is light. "So, my name means strong tree, wisdom, and light," he said. "Quite a name! I just want to live my life in happiness. If someone notices my goodness, that is all right. I do spread kindness. That is why I am a priest. I hope my story will encourage people to donate their organs so that others can live."

RABBI RICK JACOBS

SCOTT TAFFET'S FORMER RABBI

A JEWISH PERSPECTIVE ON ORGAN TRANSPLANTS

R abbi Rick Jacobs readily acknowledges that his interpretation of Jewish law may differ with many of his fellow Jews. He is affiliated with Reform Judaism which is commonly perceived as the "liberal" end of the Jewish spectrum. It is characterized by modern approaches to worship which include the full and equal participation of women in Jewish life and an abiding commitment to the pursuit of social justice. "It's a fair statement that in just about any area of Jewish life, there are some things where there is general consensus and other things less so. There may be some in the ultra-Orthodox Jewish community who would take issue with some of what I believe," he said, "but when it comes to organ donation, I think the preponderance of Jewish sages and respected deciders of Jewish law would come on the side of support of organ donation, would say it is a mandated part of our tradition."

To illustrate his belief, Rabbi Jacobs cites the decision of his friend and colleague, Rabbi Yitz Greenberg, and his wife, Blu Greenberg, whose son, J.J., died in Israel. Rabbi Greenberg is an

Orthodox Jew (commonly perceived as the "conservative" end of the Jewish spectrum). Blu Greenberg is the president of the Jewish Orthodox Feminist Alliance. J.J. was thirty-four years old at the time of his death. The Greenbergs gave permission for their son's organs to be donated. They met four of the six recipients who included a Palestinian man who received J.J.'s liver. Prior to the transplant, the man was close to death. When the Greenbergs met the recipient of what had been their son's liver, he was surrounded by his wife and seven children who were reported to be in tearful gratitude. Rabbi Greenberg said, "In Israel, you get a transplant by your priority on the waiting list, not based on being Jewish or Arab. All human beings are in the image of God and infinitely valuable. The medical system knows no politics. J.J. was like that, too. He had this tremendously generous spirit, constantly giving of himself."

"J.J. came from a very respectable Orthodox family," Rabbi Jacobs said. "I believe his organs were donated because it was the right thing to do by Jewish law and to make a point to the Orthodox community—this is not a fringe view, this is a normative, essential commitment of our tradition."

Rabbi Jacobs now serves as the president of the Union for Reform Judaism which represents an estimated 1.5 million Reform Jews in nearly nine hundred synagogues across the United States and Canada. Before taking this position, Rabbi Jacobs was the senior rabbi of the Westchester Reform Temple in Scarsdale, New York where Scott Taffet's family were members.

"I knew Scott's grandparents, parents, Scott, and his brother. Scott was a young man who grew up in the congregation," Rabbi Jacobs said. He continued to describe his relationship with the Taffets:

I had the privilege of standing under the chuppa [ceremonial Jewish wedding canopy] to officiate at his wedding. I remember his health challenges as well as his being an incredibly smart, thoughtful, caring young man who wanted nothing more than having an ordinary life, to do the things that others did with ease. There were significant challenges with his health but when Scott and Stacy stood under the chuppa, we hoped he would be able to keep his health strong, that he'd be able to be a father and husband and to do all the things he dreamt of doing. I knew him in his years before his bar mitzvah [Jewish ceremony of transition from childhood to adulthood]. He was the definition of earnest, thoughtful to those around him, not only to his family but also his peers. An impeccable human being. Religious school was not always the place that brought out the best of his peers. Many of the young men and women were not on their best behavior. I do not remember a time when Scott was not doing the right thing. Not because someone was scolding him. Not because someone was telling him, "You better do this." It's just the way he was in the world. His grandfather was the past treasurer of our synagogue, the embodiment of wise. Very considerate in judgment. Many of those qualities were passed down to Scott through his extraordinary family. He was a young man who I watched in class and admired.

His medical condition was not evident to everyone around him but I knew because I was the family's rabbi. He presented as a healthy, strong young man but knowing of his health challenges made me even more impressed. His parents shared with me his health prognosis was not expected to be positive. It was a shadow that followed him everywhere.

I was no longer at the congregation when Scott received the transplant, but I knew of it. I was so thrilled that there was a match and what Scott had always longed for—and had been so elusive—was now possible. I was relieved and cautiously delighted. One might speculate if Scott's health challenges added to his quality of decency and caring for others. He never had the luxury of taking things for granted. He was never jaded. He had every reason to be bitter, to be angry, to feel all those things someone who is facing a really tough road could feel. It was not what any of us saw.

Rabbi Jacobs believes that his beliefs and actions specific to organ donation are consistent with Jewish tradition and law.

My personal beliefs about organ transplants are deep and emphatic and, I think, in keeping with the best of the Jewish tradition. I've signed all the documents and made clear to everyone in my family, to my wife and kids, to anyone who would listen to me, if God forbid the time came early (an untimely death), I wanted them to know my wishes. It's something that needs to be asserted and quickly if my organs are to be of potential life-saving benefit to someone else. It's not an abstract concept to me. I feel very strongly that my body and my soul have been lent to me by the Holy One. If, in my death, I could bring life or sight or an extra dimension of wellness to another human being, that feels like such a high priority. Not that it would mean my family wouldn't be bereft, but it would be a powerful expression of how I tried to live my life. I think the Jewish tradition is emphatic about it.

I think sometimes Reform Judaism takes an interpretive liberty with some aspects of tradition. I also think the case is made that main Jewish legal and rabbinic codes regarding organ donation and transplantation is definitely in the category of 'to save a life.' I know of a young Jewish man killed in Israel. His organs were recovered and were given to a Palestinian. These are stories that come from a Jewish tradition that do not say 'just to save a Jewish life' but 'to save a life.' The commitment I made is that if my organs would be of benefit to anyone, the recovery of those organs for transplant would be a religious obligation.

Rabbi Jacobs reflected on the statement by ultra-Orthodox Rabbi Moshe Tendler who also serves as professor of Jewish medical ethics at Yeshiva University. Rabbi Tendler said that organ donation is not only permissible under certain circumstances, it is indeed mandatory falling under the rubric of legal obligation of Jews to preserve the lives of others. "He is one of those individuals who sets the bar for many others," Rabbi Jacobs said. He admitted that while their beliefs differ in some areas, they mostly agree on the concept of organ transplantation:

He and I would disagree on many things, but his statement gives an authentic voice of our tradition. I preached about it to my congregation. There's an ancient Jewish belief about the resurrection of the dead. There have been people who argued that if you're dead and going to be resurrected, then you better have all your organs. I say to myself, "If the Holy One can resurrect the dead, the Holy One can figure out how to give me a new kidney." Sometimes, people live in a world of superstition. I wanted to make sure that my congregation understood my belief regarding transplants. There have been people who were not emphatic with their family.

I think some people have a vague feeling that donating their organs is a good idea, but unless you take the concrete steps to convey your desire for your organs to be donated, it's likely that your wishes will not be acted upon. It would avoid—in those really horrific moments after the death of a loved one –any doubt or debate about "What did the person really want?" I hope that my congregants make sure that their desires are both written and shared with their loved ones. This includes formal declarations ranging from their driver's license to their health care proxy. I tell my congregants, "Spell it out. This is an important commitment."

When Rabbi Jacobs learned that Michel Bovill, the donor of what became Scott Taffet's lungs, was a devout Christian and that the pulmonologist who cared for Scott, Dr. Selim Arcasoy, is a Muslim, he said:

I find it nothing short of inspirational that the lungs of what had been a Christian man are now animating the life of a Jewish man and that a Muslim doctor facilitated this. I can only imagine the Holy One being overwhelmed by the beauty of humankind. That we would have such nobility within us. I made the commitment that my organs save the life of someone who needs them regardless whether the recipient is Muslim, Buddhist, Christian, or someone with whom I would have been diametrically opposed. I find the gift of life to be inspirational. In Jewish tradition, we believe that when we are born, God breathes life into us. That a devout Christian would see it as an act of faith to share their life with another is, to me, inspirational. Someone else might say, "You have the lungs that sang Christian hymns." I can imagine someone, somewhere with that hesitation. I find nothing distressing about it. That's a pure expression of genuine faith.

When hearing that the recipients of Michael's organs—who include individuals of different races, religions, and national origin—identify themselves as family with each other and Michael's family, Rabbi Jacobs said:

I am close to speechless. It's so powerful. This is the way the world was meant to be but rarely seems to be. I think of all the divisions and vitriol that tear our country and our world apart. This is a redemptive narrative. It doesn't surprise me that people of sheer goodness and nobility live in this world, live their values in this world. I hope that one day we will not make superficial judgments but see everyone created in the image of God. That we are the family of humanity. In God's world no one is a stranger. We are a human family. Stranger is how we were programmed to view the other, not how we were created to view the other.

We have these notions that our lives and the world and our souls belong to God. There's an interconnectedness to the universe. There's something interconnected with all that lives. To walk around with someone else's heart or lungs illustrates that. It's not just a spiritual question but a legal obligation. How do I live in a way that genuinely demonstrates that I am more than just a single person with a particular story but that I am a part of the larger universe? Primo Levi who survived Auschwitz [a Nazi concentration camp] wrote a book called Periodic Table. He describes the history of a molecule being the history of incarnation. Levi wrote, "Carbon, in fact, is a singular element: it is the only element that can bind in long stable chains without a great expense of energy and for life on earth precisely long chains are required. Therefore carbon is the key element of living substance." To take a spiritual view of the world, we see that all life is interconnected by design. In those moments where we don't feel our separateness, but we feel our connection to the interconnected world, those are the moments of spiritual awakening, spiritual awareness. Sometimes, it helps us act more kindly. Other times, it is really transformative. When you see people exemplifying the best of it, I hope it inspires other people to do their part.

Rabbi Jacobs doesn't see the physicality of the human body as the location of the Divine image. "For me, there's something beyond the physical in life which can be called the spiritual, the soul," he said. "To me, that is the reflection of God."

After his successful double-lung transplant, Scott and his wife Stacy decided to become parents. Their first child was a girl, and they asked Michael Bovill's parents, John and Jilayne, permission to give her the Hebrew name Michaela to honor Michael. The Bovills approved and attended the naming ceremony where they sat with the Taffets. Rabbi Jacobs commented on the Jewish practice of naming a child with the name of a dead relative:

Having performed many naming ceremonies in my rabbinic career, you're not only honoring the memory with the naming. We talk of the qualities of the person whose name is being passed on. You talk about those qualities that you so admired in that person that we pray will come with the gift of a naming. We hope and pray that those qualities will be a part of this new child's life. It's not just the name but something of that person's essence that you hope comes with that name.

"What can we do to raise the awareness of concrete ways that will bring life-healing hope to others in the world? That feels like the mission of the Jewish tradition . . . and probably close to the missions of many faith traditions. Life and everlasting life. That in our lives on earth we exemplify the best of our tradition's values."

DEA SOENT

SENIOR MONK

A BUDDHIST PERSPECTIVE
ON ORGAN DONATION
AND TRANSPLANTS

D ea Soent, the senior monk of the Korean Buddhist Bul Kwang Temple (Tappan, New York), offered this metaphor about his decision to be an organ donor: "Skin and eyes and all that junk, they can have all of it. It's just like a car. Would you care if somebody took the wheels off your car when you're done with it? No! This body is just a vehicle. The body is just going to rot but this spirit, this animation, is never going to die."

Dea Soent's birth name was Carl Haycock. He was born in Phoenix, Arizona. His mother, a practicing Catholic, sent him to parochial school. At the age of six, he became an altar boy. "I liked it, being in church," he said. "It was sort of fun. A lot of kids didn't like it. I liked it! I also come from a military family so the monk's life suits me. It's a lifestyle, like a fireman or policeman. People fall into things that suit them, that make them happy. I've been a monk for twenty-five years. I have no intention to change because it suits me."

His beliefs about organ donation and transplanting are rooted in the Zen Buddhist tradition, but his background is far broader:

> *I spent most of my life studying religion. Most of the differences [between religions] have nothing to do with the fundamental philosophy. Even in our Buddhism, in Korea there are at least sixty sects but the underlying philosophy is the same. The Buddhism that I represent is Korean and its line comes from India, then China, and arrived in Korea about 1,800 years ago. It is the Zen tradition which ascribes to the belief that everyone can become Buddha in this lifetime.*
>
> *Zen tradition is not about following rules. It's about using your wisdom to determine each situation as it exists in the moment. For instance, we take vows not to kill. But in certain instances, if people are hungry or threatened, monks have been known to go to war. Buddhist monks went to war to defend Korea against the Japanese in the fourteenth century. And if it wasn't for the monks, Korea would have been under Japanese control. So, the monks killed in order to protect their country. During the Vietnam War, Buddhist monks lit themselves on fire to protest the war. This is against the rules but they were, in a sense, doing it for the good of all people. We are trying to save all people from suffering and accept those consequences we make by our decisions. So, what do you do if a little rabbit goes running by and a hunter asks you, "Which way did the rabbit go?" Even though we take vows not to lie, maybe we're trying to save the life of the rabbit. So we might say, "I don't know." And that's a lie. Or we may help the hunter find the rabbit if we know that his family is hungry. In Buddhism, you will have many contradictory stories, but the bottom line is "How can I help this world?" We try to help people. Not myself but all people. When I wake up in the morning, I ask myself, "Why do I eat?" and the answer is to help this world. Fundamentally, this is what Buddhism is about.*

One of my favorite stories is about Buddha lifting a glass of water to his lips. He turns to his monks and says, "You must understand when you are drinking this water, you are killing millions and millions of living things." And then he drinks the water. He had no microscope. No idea what bacteria was. But through his wisdom, he knew you have to stay in a compassionate mode all the time. When I walk along the floor, God knows how many microbes I kill. You have to be aware that this is how life is and have a compassion for all living things.

He pointed to one of the images displayed in his temple. It was of a god with many heads and many hands.

The many hands represent the many ways you can help and the many heads represent the many ways to look at the world. For instance, if someone cuts you off on the freeway, you might get mad at the other driver for cutting you off. But the other driver may have someone sick in their car and is rushing to get to the hospital. So, you have to continue to look at all the views. You have to take another person's view all the time to see it from another angle. This is what we call compassion. Everyone is suffering in some way. We take a vow to save all beings from suffering.

His experience with organ donation is personal. Before becoming a monk, he was the father of a daughter who was born brain dead due to oxygen deprivation during pregnancy. She lived for two and a half years. When she passed away, "I gave her whole body away to be used as needed. All her organs were good. So, I hope it did some good in the world. I hope it helped relieve other people of their suffering."

In his Zen Buddhist tradition, he explained:

There is no opinion. No moral code. It is all cause and effect. Every action has a reaction. Every effort has a reward. If you do bad things, you get bad rewards. If you do good things, you get a good reward. All that you can do is the best you can with the wisdom you have. From the young man dying in a motorcycle accident [Michael Bovill], we have all these vital organs. If his heart goes into someone who is about to die and his parents are happy about that, we can say that this is a good result. I say it's a good result because us humans like to live. We think living is good and dying is bad. But everybody is going to die so why do we label it "bad?" It's just a label. It's just a word. So, to say it's a good thing or a bad thing, it's just my opinion. It's just a result. So, in Buddhism, we try not to make good and bad. Good and bad creates problems. Buddha said that the ultimate human condition is equanimity. Equanimity is enlightenment. It's not good. Not bad. It's just a result of cause and effect. So, my opinion of organ transplant? It's not good or bad. It's a result. If people are happy and continue to live and use this organ to continue to examine their lives and reach the point of equanimity—I guess we could label that 'good." But it could be bad. What if the person receiving the organ turns out to be rotten and goes out and kills one hundred people? Who knows what's going to happen? Maybe the person should have died. We're not God-like—so we don't know the answer. Desire causes suffering and we seek balance because once we achieve a state of balance, suffering stops.

When he learned that the recipients of Michael's organs were different genders, religions, and races, he said, "I think it's cool. I am of the same essence as every other human being on this planet. Buddhism is not a faith-based religion. It's a philosophy. Buddhism's fundamental thing is, 'Who am I? What am I? Why am I here?' In Buddhism, we ask you to believe nothing. Buddha means 'awake.' In Buddhism, there is no God." He further explained the fundamentals of Buddhism:

Inside of you, you know what's best for you. Cats know cats' jobs. Dogs know dogs' jobs. Deer know deer jobs. Alligators know alligators' jobs. Human beings are the only beings who don't know what to do with themselves. It's a fundamental problem with human beings because they have this kind of consciousness. And this consciousness makes people the only ones who can relieve suffering. The four noble truths are: life involves suffering; desire is suffering; liberation is freedom from desire; liberation comes from the Eightfold Path. Those are right view, right action, right effort, right speech, right livelihood, right concentration/ meditation, right resolve, right conduct.

These Buddhist practices directly impact Dea Soent's beliefs about the donation and transplant of human organs. "It can be beautiful, a kind of affirmation of life."

He pointed out that in the hundreds of thousands of years of human existence, it is only within decades that transplanting human organs is even possible:

Nowadays, you can get new hearts and livers. This whole idea of living in general and keeping people alive until they are in their nineties is new. For most of human time, when grandpa couldn't keep up, they left him. And grandpa was cool with it. He didn't squawk. They left him with some water and he just died. You have to keep the big picture of how human life has been. I think it's fantastic that transplants happen and I hope the recipients do good in the world. I hope they don't give some crazy guy a heart [laughs]. I'm sure the recipients have a lot of gratitude and gratitude helps people to be nicer. When you're grateful, it's hard to be mean.

Dea Soent reported that if a member of his temple told him they were going to donate their organs, "I would have nothing to say. It's a small thing. It would be the same thing as saying, 'Should I give my groceries to somebody else?' The body is not bad and it's not that important."

In Buddhism, you take responsibility for yourself. There is no victim. Everything that happens to you is the result of cause and effect. If you don't accept this, you'll live your life in fear and fear is terrible. If no fear exists, you're free. Free from life and death. Doesn't mean you're not going to die. It just means you're not afraid of it.

In addition to his duties as senior monk at his temple, Dea Soent works in a nursing home five day a week "taking care of people who are trying to live another day . . ." His descriptions point to how much those people need help and attention:

It's fear based. You got fourteen bags. You got three nurses. You can't clean yourself. You can't feed yourself. You can't wash yourself. For Christ's sake! And it's costing you ten grand a month. The money could have been better spent on the grandchildren. I don't know. We have developed a market where people have become commodities in their old age for other people to get rich on. Why are you continuing this? You're not going to get better! The only way you leave is if you die or can't pay your bill because they'll kick you out in a heartbeat if you can't pay your bill. They gave a ninety-six-year-old man a hip transplant just because they could. And somebody got paid. This is what I wrestle with. Because it confuses me.

If I ask you to stand on this two-by-four on the ground, you'd be able to balance. It'd be nothing. But if I put the two-by-four up two thousand feet in the air, you will freak out! What causes that? You had no problem standing on it when it was on the ground. But when it's two thousand feet in the air, you'd be in a whole different state. What happened to the confidence? I put myself on the two-by-four all day long because it's what I'm working on.

He summed up his perspective on organ donations and transplants. "People helping other people. For me, it's just awe. The whole idea that we can do this. That it works. It's all awe for me. Awe is a description of taking your breath away."

SHAYKH OF THE JERRAHI MOSQUE

AN ISLAMIC PERSPECTIVE ON ORGAN DONATIONS—WHAT HE REFERS TO AS "SACRIFICE"

When Yurdaer Doganata, shaykh of the Jerrahi Mosque (Chestnut Ridge, New York) was asked for an interview to explore "an Islamic perspective on organ donations," his first response was a gentle and polite "no." He did offer to look into finding another Muslim cleric who felt comfortable with addressing the topic. Within a few minutes, however, he changed his mind and gently and politely agreed to meet for the interview.

He explained his initial reservations to speak about transplants:

In the Islamic tradition, we respect scholars, and scholars who investigate a situation. There is a methodology about how to deliver a ruling in religious jurisprudence. I am not educated in that, and do not claim that I am a scholar. I am a guide who teaches that in order to become a better human being, we have to learn the essence of our religion and to be selfless. I teach how to fight against our greatest enemy, our ego and egotism.

We apply our interpretations of jurisprudence to our lives, but we do not pass judgment or expect others to follow our interpretation. We learn from the lives of all the prophets beginning with the Prophet, Adam, and from the revelations given to Prophet Mohammed, and from revelations given to other prophets, as well as the teachings of our own teachers, our shaykh. We follow the chain of teachers who connect us to the Prophet Mohammed. In this chain, we rely on the teaching of our teachers, but we don't go out and pass a religious ruling. I am a teacher for my small community here. I help them with spiritual matters and I help them to find answers to their questions. My reservation in speaking about this subject is that I didn't want to claim that I have the authority to make a formal declaration on the subject. But at the same time, because this is not a formal declaration or a religious edict, this is an unofficial interpretation of what we understand of the subject, I decided I should share what I know and how I feel. To address this topic and any other, we must understand the essence of how the prophet lived his life, how he conducted himself, and how God wanted us to conduct ourselves as human beings.

With this proviso, Shaykh Doganata elaborated on how his practices and beliefs, including the question of organ donation, are informed under the larger question of how human beings should conduct themselves. He cited, "Our book, the holy Qur'an, which we consider the word of God, teaches 'If one saves the life of another, it is like saving the life of all of humanity. If one takes the life of another, it is like killing the whole of humanity.'"

Shaykh Dognata explains further:

In Islam, there is a very strong emphasis on sacrificing what we love, those things that make us comfortable, for the benefit of others. Self-sacrifice for the benefit of others is greatly valued in

Islam. Before we do anything or say anything in this life, be it organ transplant or anything, we must first think if it is going to benefit us and others. If the answer is yes, then we must do it. If it is only going to benefit us, but not benefit others, then we must not do it. If we do or say things for our personal interest only, which do not benefit others, we refrain from doing it. Ultimately, if we do something that is not beneficial to us but is beneficial to others, it is the best action on the path to becoming a better human being.

The shaykh offered two views of Islamic scholarly opinion about organ transplants:

I am obliged to offer both, and then what we [his congregation and those who subscribe to that practice] do. It is unanimously accepted that the body is sacred. It doesn't belong to us. It is entrusted to us in this temporal life. Based on this, one view argues that we do not have the right to cut it, to split it, and to donate parts of it, because it is not ours. This opinion, however, did not find general scholarly acceptance, but a few scholars argued that organ transplants should not be permitted. They refer to what the Prophet said about not breaking the bones of the deceased, because it is as if you are breaking the bones when the person was alive. But this has nothing to do with organ transplant. This has to do with respecting the deceased and honoring the body of the deceased. This is not consistent with the verse which emphasizes that saving one life is like saving all humanity. It is clearly our responsibility as human beings to help others and to save others, and based on this, many scholars of Islam gave permission and encouragement for organ donation and transplant.

He stated that this permission is based on several conditions being met:

"It is not blind permission. The first condition is that the organ is not something that may be sold. This has to do with honoring the body that is entrusted to us by God. In that sense, we cannot sell something that does not belong to us. We should only use it to serve the most compassionate, most merciful God."

According to Islamic perspective, the word 'donor' is not quite appropriate, because it implies that we are giving away something that we possess to someone else. This is not acceptable because the body is not our possession. It is God's possession. It is not really a donation. When the soul was created, the bodies are given to the souls for the purpose of knowing God on the face of the earth, where His beautiful qualities are manifested. We need our bodies to witness His beautiful manifestations. The body has a purpose to witness His greatness. Souls were created before the body, and then the bodies were entrusted to us to fulfill our responsibilities. In other words, our souls are given their bodies to learn divine wisdom, science, divine compassion, divine artistry, divine justice. The earth is like a mirror, where His Divine attributes are reflected.

Specific to organ donation, we consider giving our organs to help others is a selfless act that brings us closer to God, and helps us to become better human beings. We all carry an entity within us that is divine and directly from Him, which is our soul. So, helping another human being is like helping God. We say feeding the hungry is like feeding God, even though God does not get hungry. Loving God's creation is loving God. And if you don't love God's creation, you cannot say, "I love God." These are fundamental principles.

If there is a necessity, certain rules can be broken. If it is about saving a life, which could be your own life, something that is not permitted or prohibited, becomes permissible. Necessity is an important condition. As an example, anything that blurs your vision or blocks your mind is forbidden. This is because as human beings, we are here to witness His divinity and anything that blurs the mind obstructs reasoning; without reasoning one cannot be a witness. That's why alcohol is forbidden in Islam. Using drugs is forbidden because it also blurs the mind. But, if you're about to freeze to death, and the only way to survive is to drink cognac, then it is permissible to drink it. If you're about to starve to death and there is only pork for you to eat—and Muslims are forbidden to eat pork—you can eat pork. Under dire conditions and when there is a necessity, something that was forbidden can become legitimate. So, one of the arguments of Islamic scholars is that saving a life is a necessity, so donating organ must be permissible. In addition to this being my religious belief, it is also my personal belief as well.

We are really not talking about organ donation. We talk about sacrifice: sacrificing from what is entrusted to us for the sake of others. Opposing organ donation would be a contradiction to the teachings, the essence of Islam. I have praised many people who have donated their kidney to save the life of another. This is a sacrifice.

Other conditions include the prohibition that a recipient cannot buy an organ from another person. And the one making the sacrifice must give full permission. It must not be enforced. It should be done willingly with no obligation. If the one making the sacrifice is alive, permission must be obtained from that person. If the one making the sacrifice has died, permission must be obtained from family members.

God could have forced every one of us to worship Him, but He gave us the freedom to choose Him as our God. That's the value of being human. Compelling any religious practice or belief is forbidden in Islam. We invite.

The fact that so many religions have the same basic beliefs [specific to organ donations and transplants] is not surprising to me. We believe that since the beginning of time, that there was *one God and one message. We believe that starting with Adam, God's message has been delivered and propagated by 124,000 prophets, and we only know the names of twenty-six. There are an incredible number of prophets and sages who have delivered the same message to the whole of humanity. We believe the message that was sent to the Prophet Muhammed. We believe the same message was sent to Abraham, Moses, and Jesus. We make no differentiation. The message contains the same fundamental truth found in Islam, Judaism, and Christianity. We are all children of the same God. It would be ridiculous to claim there is a separate God for Jews, a separate God for Christians, and a separate God for Muslims. There is one message and one humanity. We don't say the word "convert" when someone embraces Islam, we say that person remembers the only truth that was revealed. We don't believe in conversion. We believe in remembering. We should all agree that God's message was given to all of us and God doesn't conflict with Himself.*

We don't recognize this [that all humans belong to a single family] until there are events like this—the donation and transplanting of organs. God has these incredible ways of teaching us that we are one family. I see organ donation and transplant as one of the ways He teaches us. Organs don't have religions. Chairs, tables, animals don't have religions. Human beings have religions. And religion can be a way for us to learn that we are one single family. How can we deny the fact that we are all connected? For political and economic reasons, we selfishly exclude others. My happiness or comfort should not bring unhappiness or discomfort to you. You should not raise your status or economic level at the price of someone else. This is common sense, isn't it? And God, the ultimate teacher, creates circumstances—for instance, through organ donations— where someone who had been a stranger is now a member of your family.

I am the shaykh of this community. As the shaykh, I am the spiritual leader. It is not a title or position. It is a responsibility. If someone from my mosque came to me and said they were considering sacrificing an organ or organs, and asked me for guidance, I would praise them for the willingness to sacrifice for the benefit of another, and I would approve his or her request under two conditions. One, the organs could not be sold. And two, this sacrifice should not destroy the person and his or her ability to carry out his or her responsibilities. If it was being done lovingly and willingly, with consciousness of helping another human being, I would praise that person.

SWAMY SRIKRISHNA DESIKA JEEYAR

A HINDU PERSPECTIVE ON ORGAN DONATION AND TRANSPLANT

Swamy Srikrishna Desika Jeeyar, spiritual leader of the Sri Ranganatha Temple in Pomona, New York, spoke about basic Hindu beliefs and a remarkable discrepancy between beliefs and their actual practice by Hindus. (Swamy—which means "monk"—is referred to as "Swamyji.")

Our principle is non-violence. We [Hindus] are supposed to all be vegetarians. No killing of any animal, no meat, no fish, no chicken, no egg. No meat eating at all. But sixty percent of people who follow our religion do not follow this.

Second belief of our religion is no alcoholic drinking. But ninety percent of Hindus do not follow that.

Third, you can have a married life. You can have sexual contact but only under marriage. But eighty percent of Hindus have pre-marital and extra-marital affairs.

Fourth, you must always tell the truth. But ninety-nine percent of Hindus do not always speak the truth. If someone only

tells the truth, others call him an idiot. They say, "He doesn't
know how to live in this world."

Finally, our religion says we should not engage in gambling,
betting on horse races, making easy money. But more than ninety
percent of Hindus do.

Despite the disconnect between beliefs and practice, Swamyji
maintains a positive perspective. "There are some good people. I'm
not saying all are bad. Be happy that there are forty percent who
are vegetarians. Be happy that ten percent do not drink alcohol. Be
happy that twenty percent are faithful in their marriages. Be happy
that some tell the truth and do not gamble," he said. "But honestly,
the majority of people in our religion do not follow its beliefs.
I feel sad about this."

Swamyji pointed out that these are practices which accompany
the basic beliefs, but, at its core, Hinduism is "a God-centered
religion. If you have no God, you have no religion."

When asked to speak about the Hindu perspective on organ
donation and transplants, Swamyji told these stories:

There was a demon. Demon means anyone who was a bad fellow.
Anyone who is violating the established code of conduct. Anyone
who engages in illegal and immoral things. We call them demons.

Once, there was a demon. God of Heaven went to Dadhichi,
a great sage who was always in meditation. God of Heaven said,
"I need a favor from you." Dadhichi replied, "You are the God of
Heaven and you are asking me? If I can do anything I will do."
God of Heaven said, "I need your life. You are such a great sage
that every bone in your body is saturated with religious merit.
With those bones, we can make a weapon to kill the demon."
The sage said, "Sure. Take it. What need do I have for my body?
After all, if I'm dead, I do not have any use for this body. Gladly.
Take it." Immediately Dadhichi went into a yogic trance and left

his body. The soul left the body. So they collected the bones and made a great weapon called vajra. God of Heaven used the vajra and defeated the demon.

So we have the body donation. Of course, we have the organ donation.

There was another king, Alarka, a very religious king. There was a sage who was blind. The king met the great sage and asked him, "Sir, why are you blind?" The sage said, "Because we believe in reincarnation, I fear I have done something wrong in my previous lives. So I am suffering. I am blind." Alarka said, "No problem. If someone gives you his eyes, will you take them?" The sage said, "Yes." While the king was still alive, he voluntarily gave his eyes and did a transplant. So we have eye donation.

Another great king, Sibi, he was very great for charity. There was a big eagle chasing a small dove. The eagle said to Sibi, "I want to eat the dove." The dove came and fell at the feet of the king and said, "Protect me." The king said, "Okay, I will protect you." The eagle said to Sibi, "Leave the dove for me to eat." The king said, "Sorry, I gave it protection. You cannot take it. You cannot eat it." The eagle shouted at him, "What should I do? I am hungry. I need food. I need some meat. I'm a bird." Sibi said, "What you need is food. You need meat. In that case, I will give you food." The eagle asked, "Will you give your own flesh?" The king said, "No problem." The eagle said, "At least will you give the equal weight of the dove?" The king said, "No problem. Take it." Sibi took out a balance scale and placed the dove on one side and took a knife and started cutting from his own leg and placing his flesh on the other side of the balance. But the dove was very heavy. The king was cutting and cutting and cutting but still not equal to the dove. So, he gave his whole body. He said, "I gave the dove my protection." So, we Hindus have the donation of flesh in our religion.

It [organ donation] is not a taboo [for Hindus]. Unfortunately, some Hindus are not used to it. People are not well-informed in India that even after death some parts of the body can still be used for people. The heart, the lungs, the kidneys, the eyes can be used. But now there are plenty of people who are giving organ donation. Only two days ago, I came back from India. You know what they do? Brain-dead patients, very young people, twenty, thirty years old. They have motorbike accident. They die. And some people are getting into coma. Brought to the hospital brain dead. Then the organ donation team will go and request permission of the family members and ask, "Would you like to do organ donation?" And there are some well-informed, educated people who say, "Take whatever you want. We will be happy. My child's organs can be used and give life to other people." They give their permission. The policemen come and clear from the roads by the hospital where the patient is dead to the other hospital where the organ recipient is. Even if they're one hundred miles away, every traffic comes to a standstill. The whole road is lined up with the police cars. I saw it with my own eyes. To make way for the organs.

If someone asks, I will be happy to be an organ donor. No one has asked. In fact, on my driver's license I said I would donate my organs. But at my age I don't know what part of my body will be useful.

If someone from my temple came to me and said they were considering donating their organs, I would be happy to counsel that he's doing a gem of a job. I tell them, "First, mark it on your driver's license so it will be there for people to see. Second, you get your family's consent and say what parts you are willing to donate." In front of everyone we will applaud them and garland them and then honor them.

Swamyji said that in Hindu belief there are no restrictions or reservations about the organs of a donor of one religion being transplanted into the body of someone of another race or religion. "Skin color doesn't matter at all. Segregating people based on their skin color is the greatest injustice that people have ever done to themselves. We do not segregate people based on religion or skin color. We believe that the whole of humanity is one," he said.

TIMELINE OF HISTORICAL EVENTS AND SIGNIFICANT MILESTONES OF ORGAN TRANSPLANTATION

APPROXIMATELY 800 B.C.

Indian doctors had likely begun grafting skin—technically the largest organ—from one part of the body to another to repair wounds and burns.

16TH CENTURY

Italian surgeon Gasparo Tagliacozzi, sometimes known as the father of plastic surgery, reconstructed noses and ears using skin from patients' arms. He found that skin from a different donor usually caused the procedure to fail, observing the immune response that his successors would come to recognize as transplant rejection.

1823

First skin autograft transplantation of skin tissue from one location on an individual's body to another location performed in Germany.

1869

First skin transplant performed.

EARLY 1900S

European doctors attempted to save patients dying of renal failure by transplanting kidneys from various animals, including monkeys, pigs, and goats. None of the recipients lived for more than a few days.

1905

Eduard Zirm, an Austrian ophthalmologist, performed the world's first corneal transplant, restoring the sight of a man who had been blinded in an accident.

1912

Transplant pioneer Alexis Carrell received the Nobel Prize for his work in the field. The French surgeon had developed methods for connecting blood vessels and conducted successful kidney transplants on dogs. He later worked with aviator Charles Lindbergh to invent a device for keeping organs viable outside the body, a precursor to the artificial heart.

1936

Ukrainian doctor Yu Yu Voronoy transplanted the first human kidney, using an organ from a deceased donor. The recipient died shortly thereafter as a result of rejection.

1954

Surgeons at Boston's Peter Bent Brigham Hospital transplanted a kidney from twenty-three-year-old Ronald Herrick into his twin brother, Richard. Since donor and recipient were genetically identical, the procedure succeeded.

1959

First successful kidney transplant performed between fraternal twins.

1960

First successful kidney transplant performed between siblings who were not twins.

1960

British immunologist Peter Medawar, who had studied immunosuppression's role in transplant failures, received the Nobel Prize for his discovery of acquired immune tolerance. Soon after, anti-rejection drugs enabled patients to receive organs from non-identical donors.

1962

First kidney, lung, and liver transplants recovered from deceased donors.

1963

First organ recovery from a brain-dead donor.

1966

First successful pancreas transplant performed.

1967

First successful heart transplant performed in South Africa. Surgeon Christiaan Barnard replaced the diseased heart of dentist Louis Washkansky with that of a young accident victim. Although immunosuppressive drugs prevented rejection, Washkansky died of pneumonia eighteen days later.

First simultaneous kidney/pancreas transplant performed.

First successful liver transplant performed.

1968

The Uniform Anatomical Gift Act (US) drafted by the National Conference of Commissioners on Uniform State Laws, established the uniform donor card as a legal document of gift in all fifty states; identified the types and priority of individuals who could donate a deceased person's organs; and enabled anyone over eighteen to legally donate his or her organs upon death.

First (US) organ procurement organization was established, New England Organ Bank based in Boston.

First definition of brain death based on neurological criteria developed by a Harvard Ad Hoc Committee.

First successful bone marrow transplant performed.

1976

Discovery of cyclosporine's ability to suppress the immune system, helping to prevent the rejection of transplanted organs.

1980

Uniform Determination of Death Act (US) defines death as either irreversible cessation of circulatory and respiratory functions or irreversible cessation of all functions of the brain, including the brain stem.

1981

First combined heart/lung transplant performed.

1983

First successful single lung transplant with significant recipient survival (more than six years) takes place in Canada.

The Food and Drug Administration (US) approves cyclosporine, which can improve transplant outcomes as its immunosuppressive qualities lessen the potential for organ rejection.

1984

As transplants became less risky and more prevalent, Congress (US) passed the National Organ Transplant Act to monitor ethical issues and address the country's organ shortage. The law established a centralized registry for organ matching and placement to ensure fair and equitable allocation of donated organs; outlawed the sale of human organs; established the Scientific Registry of Transplant Recipients to conduct an ongoing evaluation of the scientific and clinical status of organ transplantation; provided for grants for the establishment, initial operation, and expansion of organ procurement organizations.

1986

The Omnibus Budget Reconciliation Act of 1986 (US) required hospitals to have in place policies for offering all families of deceased patients the opportunity to donate their loved one's organs.

The first contract for establishment and operation of the Organ Procurement and Transplantation Network is awarded by the US Department of Health and Human Services to the United Network for Organ Sharing. OPTN provides services for equitable access and allocation of organs and sets the membership criteria and standards for transplant centers in the US.

First successful double lung transplant, which was performed in Canada.

1987

Medicare (US) pays for heart transplants performed at hospitals that meet criteria set by the Health Care Financing

Administration (now Centers for Medicare and Medicaid Services).

First successful intestine transplant performed.

1988

First split-liver transplant surgery—performed in France. This procedure enables two recipients to each receive a portion of one donated liver.

1990

Nobel Prize awarded to Dr. Joseph E. Murray and Dr. E. Donnall Thomas, pioneers in kidney and bone marrow transplants, respectively. Dr. Murray performed the first successful kidney transplant (1954) and Dr. Thomas performed the first bone marrow transplant (1968).

Medicare (US) pays for liver transplants (that meet specific medical criteria) performed at approved hospitals.

1995

First living donor kidney was removed through laparoscopic surgical methods that result in a small incision and easier recovery for the donor.

1996

US Congress authorizes mailing organ and tissue donation information with income tax refunds (sent to approximately seventy million households).

1998

First successful hand transplant—performed in France.

The Centers for Medicare and Medicaid Services (US) issued its Hospital Conditions of Participation in Medicare and Medicaid programs requiring participating hospitals to refer all deaths and imminent deaths to the local organ procurement organization.

1999

Organ Donor Leave Act (US) was passed by Congress to allow federal employees to receive paid leave and serve as living organ or marrow donors.

2001

Number of living donors exceeds number of deceased donors for the first time in the US.

2002

Department of Health and Human Services (US) premieres its new documentary, *No Greater Love*. This hour-long film, narrated by Angela Lansbury, depicts the power of transplantation and the critical need for more donors.

Up-to-the-minute data on the number of people waiting for organ transplants in the United States are now available online through the Organ Procurement and Transportation Network.

2003

The Organ Donation Breakthrough Collaborative was launched by the US Department of Health and Human Services to increase donation in the nation's largest hospitals by implementing an intensive and highly focused program to promote widespread use of best practices. In 2005, transplant centers joined the initiative with the goal of increasing the number of organs per donor. A revised version of the program continues today as the Donation and Transplantation Community of Practice.

2005

Baltimore's Johns Hopkins Hospital pioneered the "domino chain" method of matching donors and recipients. Willing donors who are genetically incompatible with their chosen recipients are matched with strangers; in return, their loved ones receive organs from other donors in the pool.

First successful partial face transplant—performed in France.

2006

Institute of Medicine (IOM) released a new report, "Organ Donation: Opportunities for Action." The IOM examined the ethical and societal implications of numerous strategies to increase donation and considered several ethical issues regarding living donation, resulting in the presentation of seventeen recommendations for action.

2010

Spanish doctors conducted the world's first full face transplant on a man injured in a shooting accident. A number of partial face transplants had already taken place around the world.

2014

In the US, vascularized composite allographs (VCAs) is added to the definition of organs covered by federal regulation and legislation (the National Organ Transplant Act). VCAs involve the transplantation of multiple structures that may include skin, bone, muscles, blood vessels, nerves, and connective tissue.

Source:

https://organdonor.gov/about/facts-terms/history.html,
https://www.history.com/news/organ-transplants-a-brief-history
http://www.donatelife.gov.au/sites/default/files/History_of_Organ_and_Tissue_Donation.pdf

PART THREE

AUTHOR'S NOTES

PERSONAL PROCESS, REFLECTIONS, AND DECISIONS REGARDING ORGAN DONATION

I clearly heard Roxanne Watson proclaim her passion for saving lives through signing up organ donors. She calls it her mission. While waiting in intensive care for more than two months—waiting to die or for a heart transplant—Roxanne committed to recruiting organ donors so that no one would have to endure what she endured. Almost ten years have passed since she received what had been Michael Bovill's heart. Roxanne currently devotes herself to almost daily engagements recruiting donors at street fairs, college student unions, funerals, and just about wherever she goes. As she spoke about her mission to save lives through signing up organ donors, I recognized that I had never seriously considered becoming a donor. Although I was moved by Roxanne's mission, I felt a visceral discomfort with the idea of *me* being a donor. Before meeting Roxanne, I had never considered it.

And I recognized a disconnect in myself. . .

For more than thirty-five years, on a daily basis, I take kitchen scraps (and ashes during cold weather from our wood-burning stove) and incorporate them into frequently turned compost piles. For several years, I operated a small commercial compost operation. I experienced awe as huge mountains of leaves, manure, and vegetable scraps transformed into far smaller piles of rich, black, odorless compost. As a forester, I have observed with awe and gratitude the miraculous process of trees generating leaves and needles which eventually fall to the earth to nurture the soil. Trees extract the minerals and water from the soil—from the leaves and other decomposing organic matter—to make more trees and leaves. I never found God inside buildings. I did find a spiritual confirmation in photosynthesis.

The Buddhist teacher, Thich Nhat Hanh said, "The banana peel does not fear the compost pile." I believe that. I have no idea if I will fear death when it calls me, but in the relative state of health I find myself today, I don't believe I fear my destination in the great compost pile in the sky or ground or water or air or ether. . . or wherever the great compost pile resides.

I love these verses from Walt Whitman's *Leaves of Grass*:

I depart as air, I shake my white locks at the runaway sun,
I effuse my flesh in eddies, and drift it in lacy jags.

I bequeath myself to the dirt to grow from the grass I love,
If you want me again look for me under your boot-soles.

Who could better express an authentic invitation to ensure that my organs be used to help someone in need? Even with Walt Whitman, Thich Nhat Hanh, and now Roxanne Watson inspiring me, I still felt a real reservation to giving permission for my organs to be recovered after my death. Given a lifelong rigorous care of my physical body, I feel confident that my organs are in a state that could benefit others. But the reservation lingered . . .

Shayk Yurdaer Doganata told me that in Islamic tradition, if someone gives permission for their organs to be recovered after their death, it is not referred to as "donation," but "sacrifice." He said that our bodies are not our own, so we cannot donate what does not belong to us. He said our bodies are on loan from Allah—that we have bodies to be of service to others. This resonated with me.

The compost (and Thich Nhat Hanh) primed me to see that the banana peel can live forever as tomatoes, grasshoppers, roses, and just about any other form of life. So, after I die (my heart stops beating, my lungs no longer inhaling and exhaling), my heart and lungs and liver and kidneys and other elements of "my" body could easily follow the banana peel into becoming elements of people who could use them; so that someone waiting in an intensive care unit could stop waiting and go on with (hopefully) a good life. My reservation wavered but didn't disappear . . .

During the time I was writing *Michael's Legacy*, I spoke with my wife of almost thirty-nine years, Anna Teigen, frequently about the people whose stories are found in this book. We spoke about how miraculous their stories are and how organ donation was an essential element in making this possible. Initially, both of us expressed reservation about our engaging in the practice. Anna said that one of her thoughts was that if I die before her, she wanted to be able to focus exclusively on her loss and my passing and be free of a potential burden of dealing with my body parts being removed. I understood and respected her wish.

Anna and I spoke about this a few times again. Eventually she said that she would respect my desire to be an organ donor—if I truly wanted to do it.

Then I asked the Dea Soent about his belief concerning organ donation, he spoke to me with a picture that I didn't expect from this Buddhist monk. He said if you have an old car that is just not worth trying to keep going and you junk it—you wouldn't feel bad if someone used the wheels that were still serviceable. I loved how graphic his response was. I agreed that I'd be happy if someone used the wheels. With that, my reservation evaporated.

A few weeks later, I went to the Department of Motor Vehicles to renew my driver's license. One of the questions on the renewal form asks if you want to become an organ donor. I checked the box marked "yes."

WHEN PEOPLE ASK IF I KNEW MICHAEL...

During the three years of writing *Michael's Legacy*, many people asked if I knew Michael. Initially, I didn't know how to answer the question even though it sounded like "yes" or "no" would be a simple—and accurate— answer. It wasn't so simple...

I met and spoke with many people who knew the living and breathing Michael. They shared intimate stories and pictures of this special human being. I became immersed in these stories and recognized a growing love for him. I met and spoke with three of the five recipients of his organs. When I spoke with Roxanne (whose heart had beaten in Michael), Scott (whose lungs had inhaled and exhaled in Michael), and Diana (whose kidney had filtered the blood in Michael), I felt that I was meeting a part of Michael.

When I was writing the manuscript, I had no idea if it would ever become a book that other people would read. I certainly hoped it would manifest as a published work that would inspire others with a true story of goodness. I continued to interview, write, and edit because I was drawn to this story and if it never got any further than that, it was still an important exploration for me.

About two years into working on the book, I dreamt that Michael spoke to me. My visual memory of the dream is dim, but I knew it was Michael. When the folks who knew him in life did impressions of his voice, I heard a consistent playful quality to his tone. Every person who knew him in life spoke of his almost ever-present, genuine smile. The Michael who revealed himself in my dream spoke with the same playful voice his friends and family mimicked and he displayed a welcoming and warm smile. I remember him saying to me, "It's good. Write the book." His confirmation was all I needed.

Before writing this book, life and death had been clearly distinct and different states to me. More and more, they became artificial constructions. Thich Nhat Hanh, the Buddhist monk and poet wrote, "Your so-called birthday is really your continuation day. The next time you celebrate, you can say, 'Happy Continuation Day'. . . If we look very deeply, we will transcend birth and death."

In coming to know Michael through stories told by friends and family; meeting Roxanne, Scott, and Diana; and Michael's appearance in my dream. I eventually had clarity. When people ask me if knew Michael, I now honestly say, "Yes."

REFLECTIONS ON WRITING
MICHAEL'S LEGACY

For the past three years, *Michael's Legacy* has been an almost constant companion. Living with this story caused my old pictures of family, life, and death to vaporize.

On the demographic surface, Michael was a white, Protestant man born in the United States. The recipients of his organs included an African American woman, a white Jewish man born in the United States, an African-American young man, a Catholic girl whose parents were born in Mexico, and a man born in China. After the transplants, these elements of what had been Michael were now animating Roxanne Watson, Scott Taffet, Diana Martinez-Moran, Elijah Parker, and Zhou Yuan Li.

The toxic dehumanizing of "the other" (individuals of racial, religious, sexual orientation, country of origin, and abilities different from our own) that infests our lives is shattered—for me—by Michael's legacy.

Thich Nhat Hanh, a Buddhist monk and teacher, speaks about "inter-being." He says that a sheet of paper is composed of sunlight, clouds, rain, soil, and even the logger who felled the tree that became the paper. Without these and many other elements—including the mother of the logger and the bread the logger ate—the sheet of paper would not exist. The sheet of paper is interdependent, interpenetrated, inter-being with the entire universe. That it is all one. This is what I've come to see through Michael and his legacy.

Stacy Taffet, the wife of Scott Taffet (who received Michael's lungs), identifies herself as Jewish. She cried as she said that in her tradition, the Hebrew name of a child is that of a dead relative and that her first-born's Hebrew name is Michaela, named for her "relative" Michael Bovill. The Taffets and Bovills had no blood relation before what had been Michael's lungs enabled Scott to lead a healthy life and able to become Michaela's father.

Kellen Wingate, the son of Roxanne Watson who was the recipient of what had been Michael's heart, spoke about now having three sisters when, before the transplant, he had been an only child. Kellen and Roxanne are African American and Kellen's "sisters" are the white daughters of Michael's family.

The doctors who worked with the recipients of Michael's organs included a woman whose parents were born in Korea; a woman who was born in India; a man born in the United States who identifies himself as Catholic; and a man who grew up in Turkey who identifies himself as Muslim. That doctor, Selim Arcasoy, who cared for Scott, who identifies himself as Jewish. The lungs of Michael, who identified himself as Christian, directly made possible the birth of Scott and Stacy's Jewish daughter, Michaela. Selim said, "Religion should not matter how we treat each other in medicine or outside of medicine. We're all human."

Jilayne Bovil, Michael's mother said, "This is not just about Michael. This is how life goes on—sharing with each other. If you don't share yourself, you won't know how to love."

Karen Gans, one of the transplant coordinators from LiveOnNY who worked with Michael, said, "From this work, I see that everything is just one. There's no divide. It's just one."

I agree.

EPILOGUE

My mother, Bella Judelson, worked as a secretary. She was untrained in counseling or therapy, and yet people came up to her in the office and told her intimate stories of their lives. All kinds of people felt safe with her—staff in her office, her supervisors, custodians, visitors. My mother listened with an open mind and an open heart. She had what Dr. Martin Luther King—whose birthday I share— referred to as "a heart full of grace. A soul generated by love." I don't know if my mother recognized her gift as a trusted listener to be a calling but that's how I now perceive it. Among other gifts I inherited from my parents, this listening and inviting the stories and words to come became one of my callings.

When I was growing up in New Haven in the 1960's—even though I didn't yet recognize this as *my* calling—stories revealed themselves and I recorded them. I co-wrote a novel, *Telling It Like It Is*, based on my experience as a white teenager attending a predominantly black high school. It was published in 1975. In 1978 and 1979, when I lived in the small Central African village of Kongbo, I started telling stories. My first "performances" were in the dominant language of the village, Sangho. When I returned to the United States, I continued to tell stories—in English.

Much of my work as a performer and writer is what I learned from my mother:

- be quiet and listen;
- be fully respectful of the person who is entrusting you with their story;
- honor honesty and
- cultivate what is affirming of life.

The quieter and more respectful I was, life-affirming stories revealed themselves to me.

The stories who revealed themselves to me were consistent with another statement by Dr. King: "When you discover what you will be in your life, set out to do it as if God Almighty called you at this particular moment in history to do it." The stories were about people who used the unique gifts and skills they possessed to act with courage when faced with violations of decency.

During the Siege of Sarajevo in 1992, the cellist Vedran Smailovic witnessed a mortar shell kill twenty-two starving people waiting in a bread line. For the next twenty-two days, Vedran played a concert in a bomb crater where the twenty-two died. Vedran was a cellist and so he played the cello to honor life. I researched Vedran's story and wrote a play called *The Open Window* which I performed sixty-three times.

In the 1980s, the Aryan Nations, a neo-Nazi, white supremacist organization, declared the states of Wyoming, Montana, Washington, Oregon, and Idaho to be site of the "White Homeland." The Federal Bureau of Investigation identified the Aryan Nations as a "terrorist threat." I believe they transcend being a "threat" and need to be recognized as "terrorist." They were directly or indirectly responsible for several racially charged incidents which took place in Billings, Montana in 1993 where Native Americans, Jews, and African Americans were targeted. Dawn Fast Horse, a Native

American woman, woke up one morning to find the Nazi symbol and the words "Die Indian" spray painted on the exterior of her home while she and her children were asleep the night before. The next day, union painters armed with ladders, paint, and brushes repainted her entire house. Skinheads entered the Wayman African Methodist Episcopal Church during a Sunday morning service in an attempt to frighten the all-black congregants. Reverend Bob Freeman led the service to its conclusion. For the next several weeks, white residents of Billings attended Reverend Freeman's church to ensure the safety of their African American neighbors. A rock was thrown through the window of a young Jewish boy, Isaac Schnitzer, who had placed a menorah, a Jewish symbol, in his window. Within days, Gary Svee, the editor of the *Billings Gazette*, printed a full-page menorah in his newspaper and invited residents to display the menorah in their windows. Residents of Billings mobilized and within days thousands of homes, churches, schools, and businesses in Billings–with a population of fifty Jews–displayed this Jewish symbol in their windows. For me, this was a story that demanded to be performed—demonstrating people doing what they could do with the resources available to them in the place where they live in the moment of need. I interviewed several of the actual heroes of Billings and crafted a play called *The King of Denmark Comes to Billings* that we performed sixteen times.

For more than a decade, students of the public schools of the East Ramapo School District (New York) have suffered a loss of educational, social, and developmental opportunities. This has been perpetrated by people whose interest is focused on supporting private, religious schools at the expense of the overwhelmingly African American and Latinx students of the public schools. Inspired by the heroic efforts of representatives of the Spring Valley NAACP and others, I interviewed many students, teachers, administrators, and members of the communities affected by the situation. Each, in their own way, stood up to the powers that be to non-violently struggle for the rights of all the students. Using their words, I crafted a script into a play called *East Ramapo*. With many of the individuals performing as themselves, we presented eleven performances.

Michael's Legacy revealed itself to me as another story where many people did what they could do with the resources they possess in the moment of need. Michael chose to be an organ donor. His parents gave their consent. The physicians and surgeons performed interventions that strike me as miracles. The transplant coordinators—in moments of tremendous grief and tension—remained calm and organized an astonishing volume of people, transportation, highly complex information, surgical suites, and procedures while gently relating to the people who loved Michael. Michael, while he was alive, modeled kindness, generosity, and service to others. His organs and legacy are animating others who are modeling their unique service to others. Michael's story grabbed me and indicated clearly that it was my job to tell it.

I did my best to exemplify another direction from Dr. King: "If it falls your lot to be a street sweeper . . . sweep streets so well that all the hosts of heaven and earth will have to pause and say, 'Here lived a great street sweeper who swept his job well.'"

My lot was not to be a preacher or street sweeper or a surgeon. My lot is to honestly tell stories who invite readers and audiences to act with kindness, courage, and decency in the moment of need.

It is presumptuous, but I believe that Dr. King and my mother approve.

ACKNOWLDGEMENTS

Willie Trotman for suggesting I interview Roxanne Watson—who opened the door to this magical story.

Art Aldrich, who has somehow kept *Our Town News*, a community newspaper, functioning and flourishing for more than forty years and who published the article about Roxanne.

Jaimen McMillan for making visible and accessible how to meet others.

Ted Kuster for his tough-love writing guidance.

Rachel Maldanado for her impeccable and generous editing.

Ken Simpson, Karin Stallard, Eleanor Zimmerman, Ellen Mead, Doris Sacks, Neil Rindlaub, Deborah Wiggs, Marissa Chin, Shelly Hollywood Palestino O'Neill, Celine Gendron, and Bob and Nancy Berkowitz for reviewing this story in its many incarnations and courageously offering their feedback.

Cynthia Manson, Nancee Adams, and Roberta Gately, publishing and writing professionals, who generously offered guidance and handholding in the baffling process of navigating the world of publishing.

Each of the people who agreed to be interviewed, reviewed the drafts, and gave their approval to include their stories in this book.

Julia Rivera, Karen Cummings, Maria Torres, Safiya Raheem, Ali McSherry, and Megan Fackler at LiveOnNY who facilitated making contact with several of the people interviewed in this book.

Julia Alamo for her thoughtful, sensitive, and insightful translation of the interviews with Diana Flores-Moran and Socorro Moran.

Jared Esselman and Steven Pollock who facilitated contact with Michael's Coast Guard shipmates.

Kailin Waterman, veteran member of the San Francisco Fire Department, for his insight into firefighters and paramedics and his good ears which helped in transcribing a delicate interview.

Bella Judelson, who modeled a love and respect for using the right words and her genuine interest in others.

Anna Teigen, the kindest person I've ever met, my dearest friend, and precious wife.

John and Jilayne Bovill for their open hearts and giving gestures.

Michael Bovill, whose service to others transcended life and death.

ABOUT THE AUTHOR

Mark Judelson's first (imagined) career was as the centerfielder for the New York Yankees when Mickey Mantle retired. Other potential jobs included— but are not limited to—following in the footsteps of his brother, Alan, a graduate of the United States Naval Academy; logging; nursing; farming; and more. Centerfield at Yankee Stadium and serving as a naval officer did not manifest, but others did.

He is a graduate of the Yale School of Forestry and Environmental Studies. Mark served as a Peace Corps volunteer in the Central African Empire, executive director of an environmental education center/farm for at-risk teenagers, and executive director of the Arts Council of Rockland. Currently, he works at the Rudolf Steiner Fellowship Community, an intergenerational community centered on the care of the elderly and the earth. He is a first-degree black belt in Tae Kwon Do; certified arborist with the International Society of Arboriculture; Level III graduate of the Spacial Dynamics Institute; and registered somatic movement therapist with the International Somatic Movement Education and Therapy Association.

Along the way, Mark discovered that stories chose him to tell them through writing and performing. His first book, *Telling It Like It Is*, a novel co-authored with Jane Roberts, is based on his experience as a white teenager attending a predominantly black high school and was published in 1975.

He wrote and performed several plays based on true stories of people who committed acts of courage and kindness in the face of violence and genocide (www.stories ofpeace.com). For this work, the Spring Valley Branch of the NAACP recognized Mark with their President's Award in 2018.

He is joyously married to Anna Teigen; father to two remarkable human beings; and grandfather to two wonderful grandchildren. Anna and Mark live in Rockland County, New York.